AF608579

Falten und Verwerfungen / Folds and Faults

Florian Neufeldt

o. T. / Untitled (2017)
Brandschutztür / fire door
210 × 87 × 53 cm

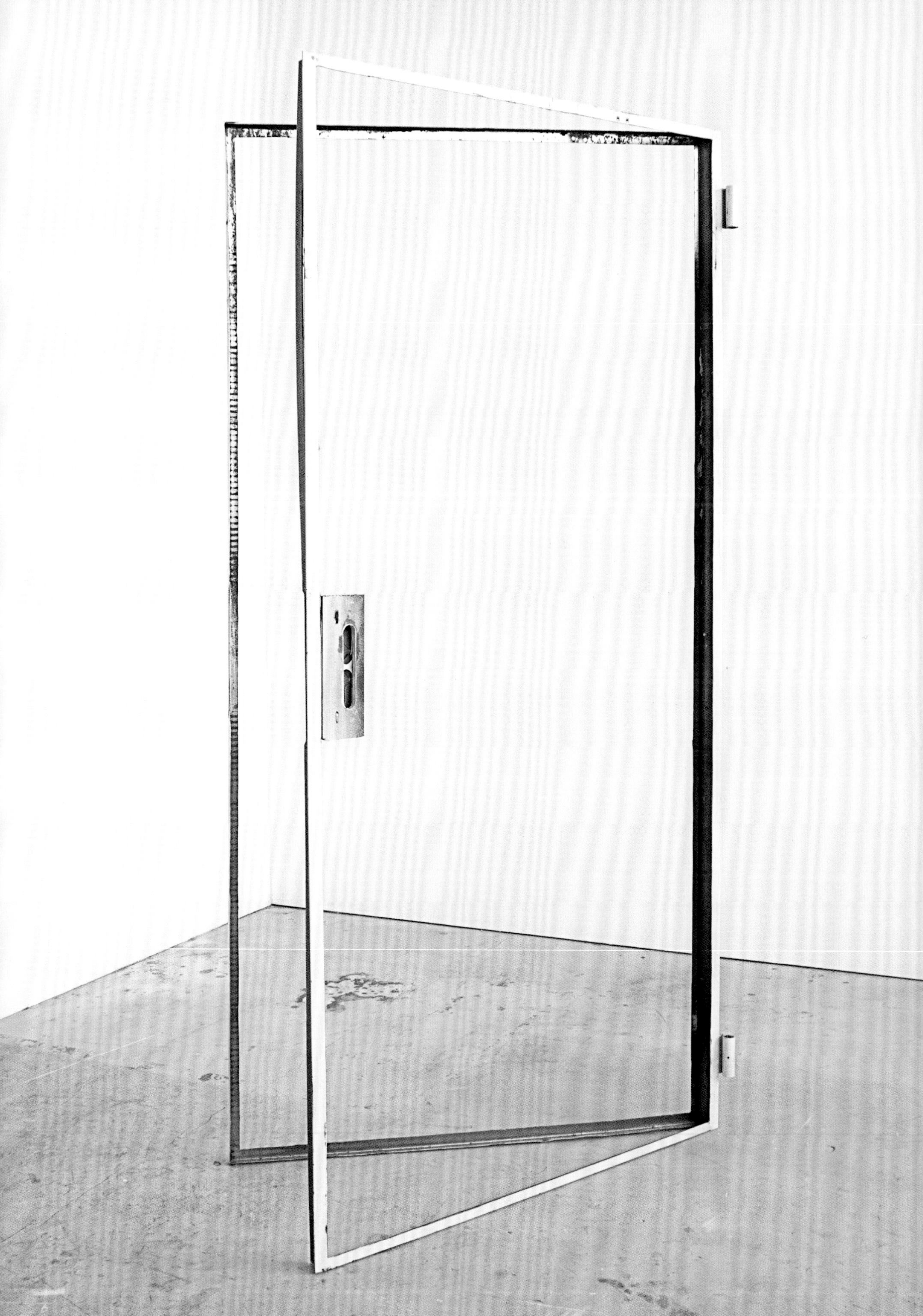

Sheets (2019)
Brandschutztüren / fire doors

Sheets (2019)
Brandschutztür / fire door
200 × 97 × 3 cm

Sheets (2017)
Brandschutztür / fire door
121 × 83 × 73 cm

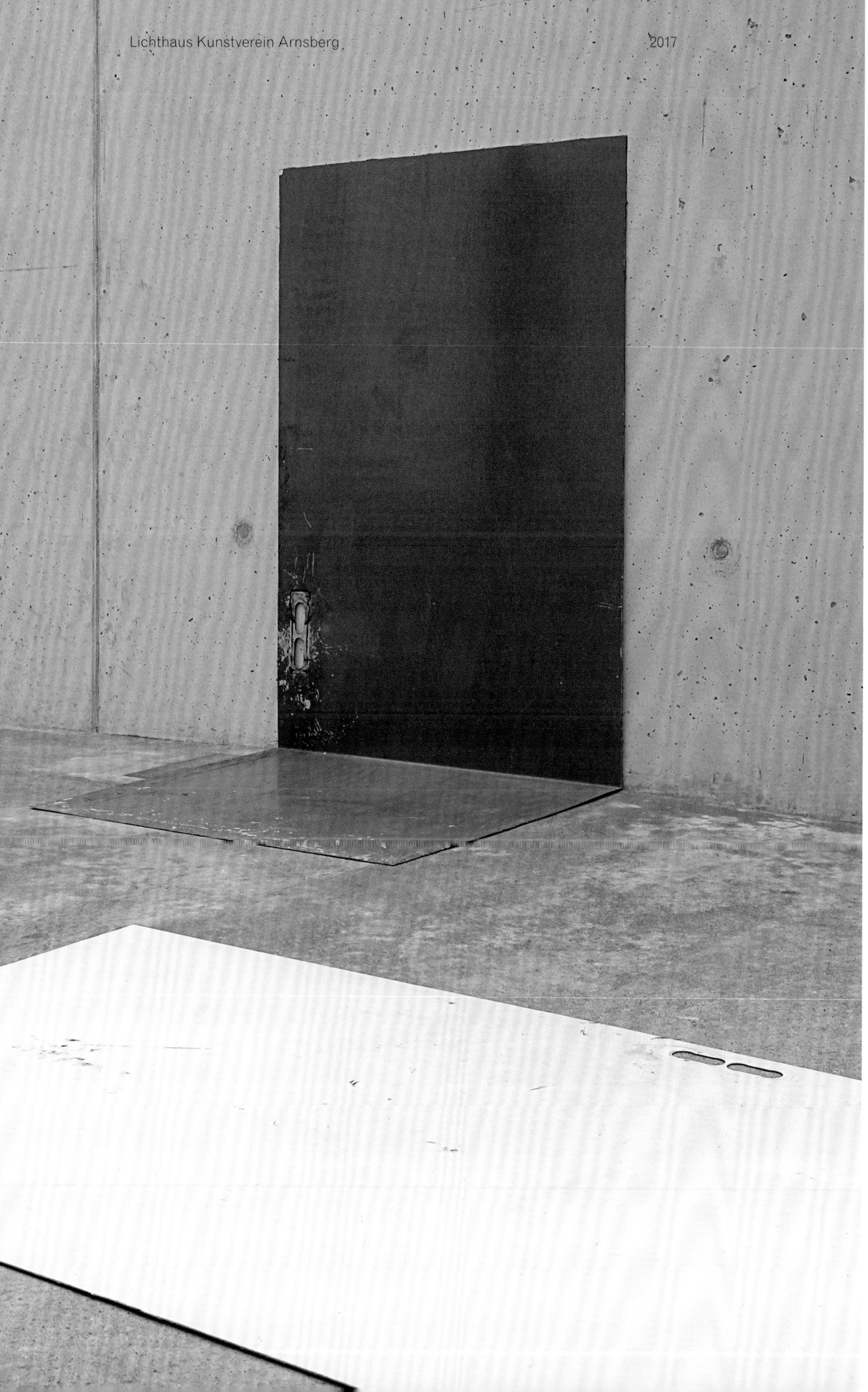

Sheets (2019)
Brandschutztür / fire door
205 × 96 × 4 cm

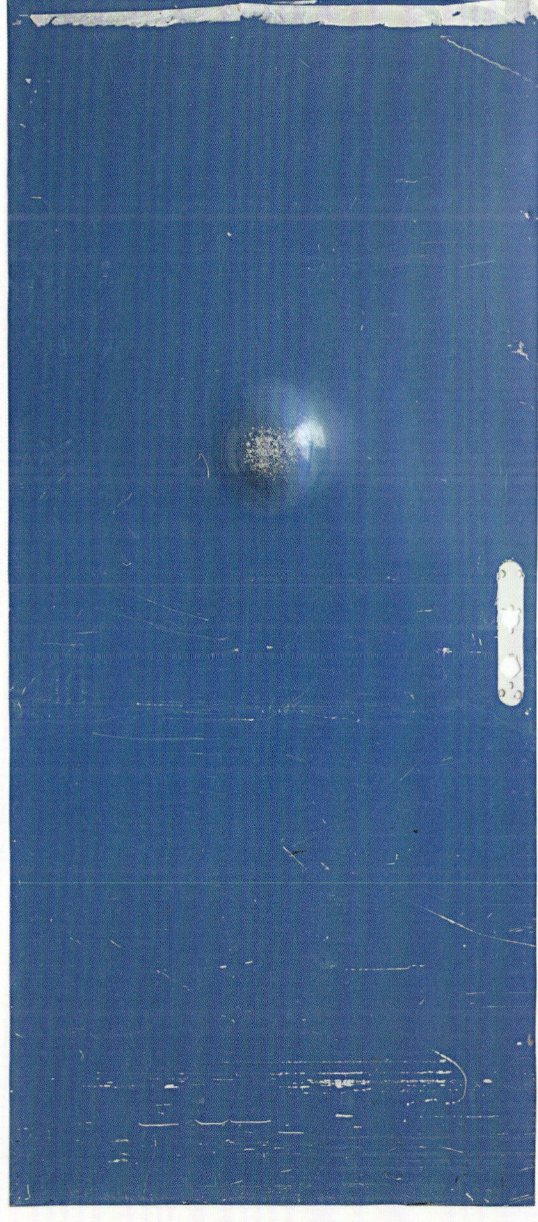

Sitzordnung / Seating Arrangement (2017)
Stuhlgestell, Wandpaneel des Ausstellungsraums /
chair frame, wall panel of the exhibition space
14 × 47 × 13 cm

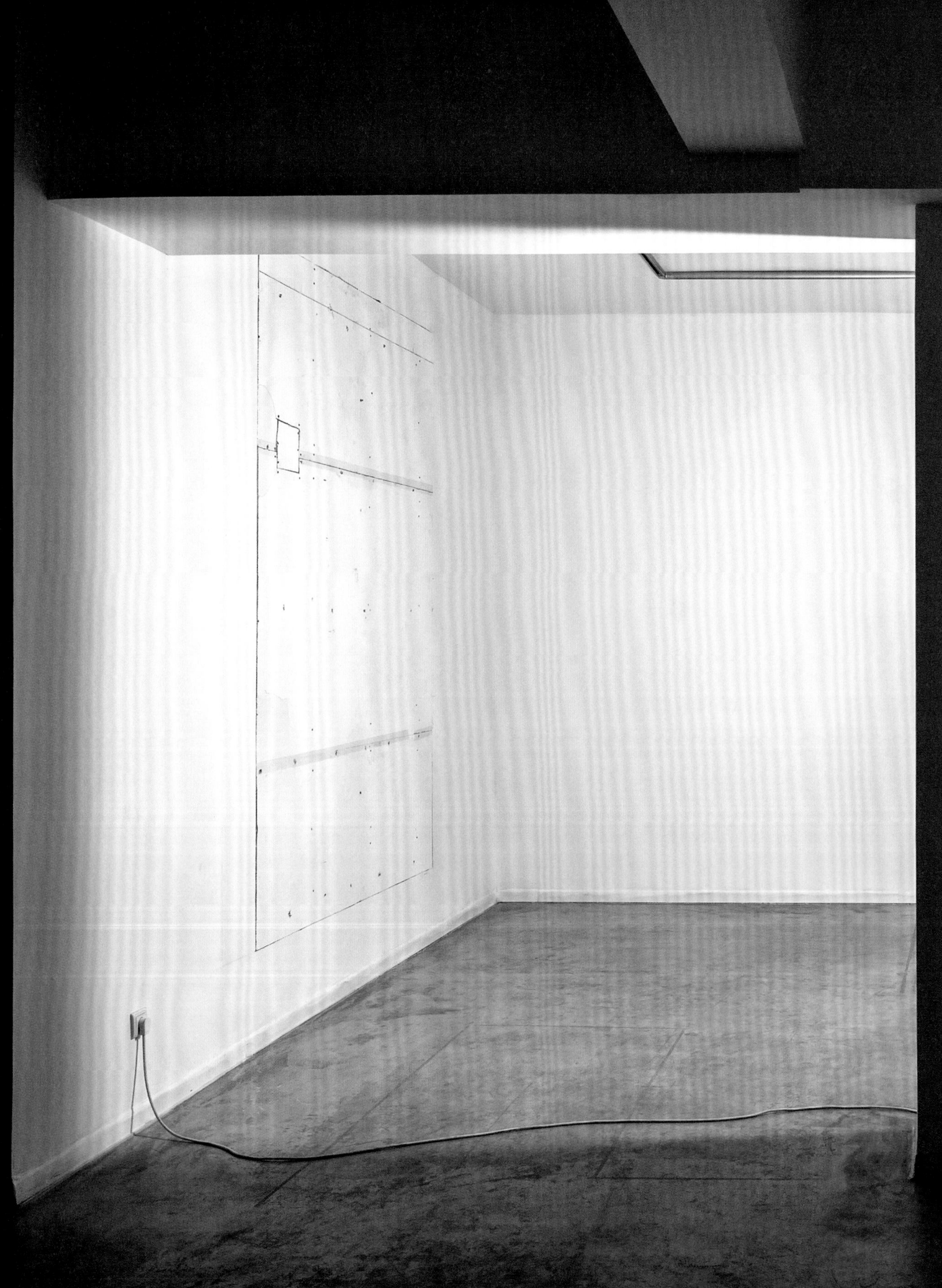

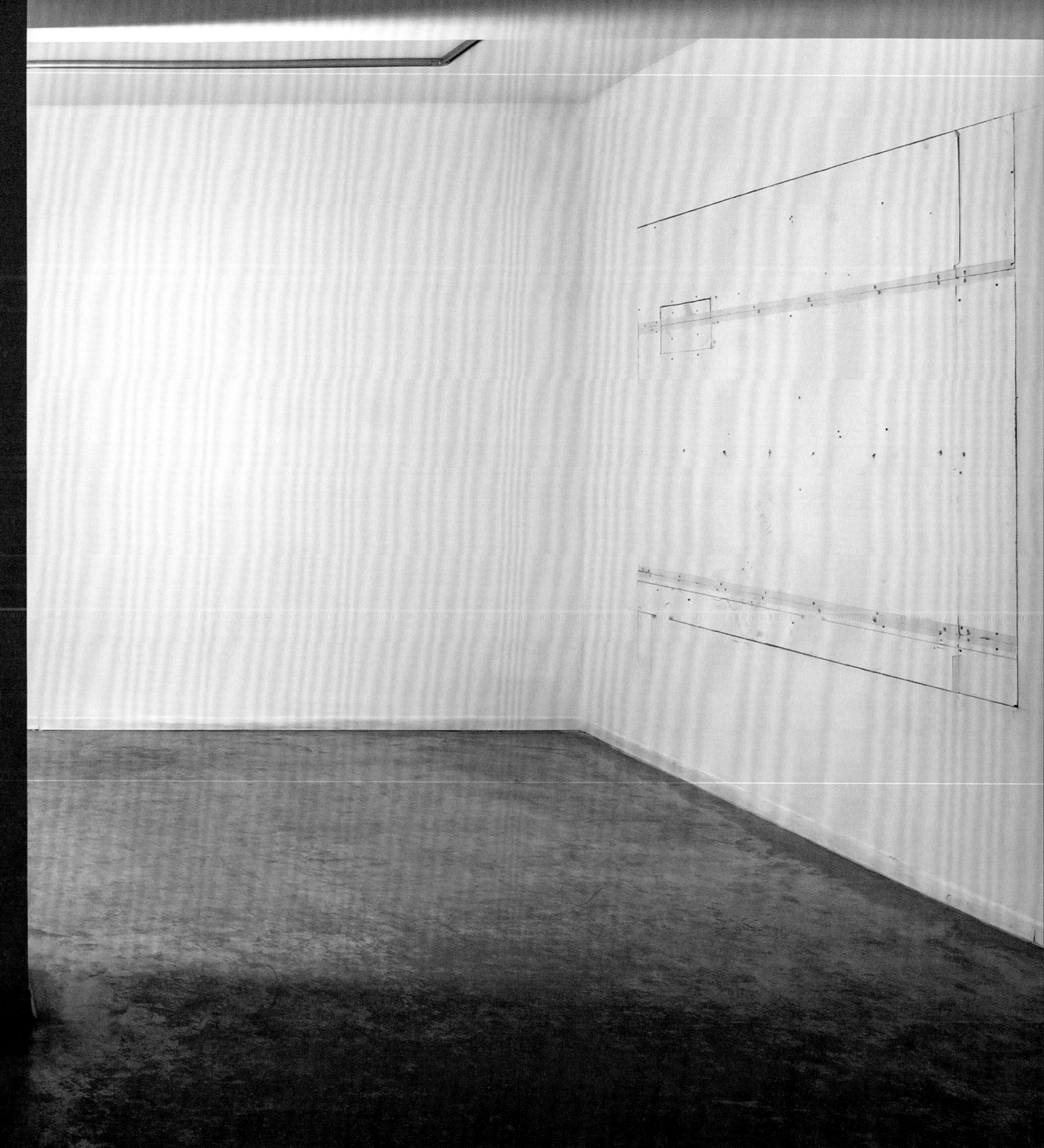

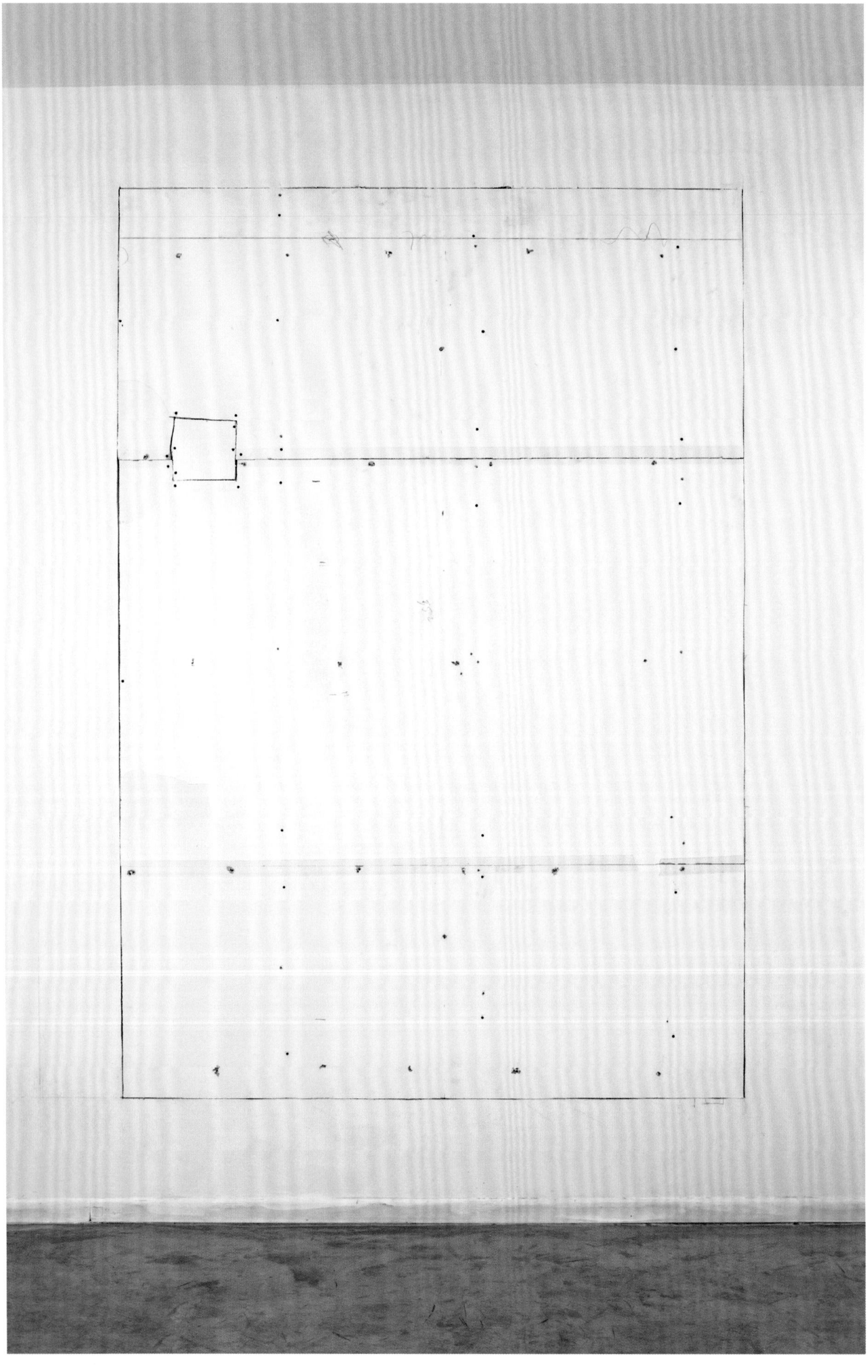

Doppelgänger (Walls With Flaws) (2013)
Gipskarton, Leuchtstofflampe / plasterboard, fluorescent lamp
270 × 190 cm (je Wandausschnitt / each wall cut)

Sealed Vessels (2018)
Gasflasche, Hühnerei /
gas bottle, chicken egg
155 × 23 × 23 cm

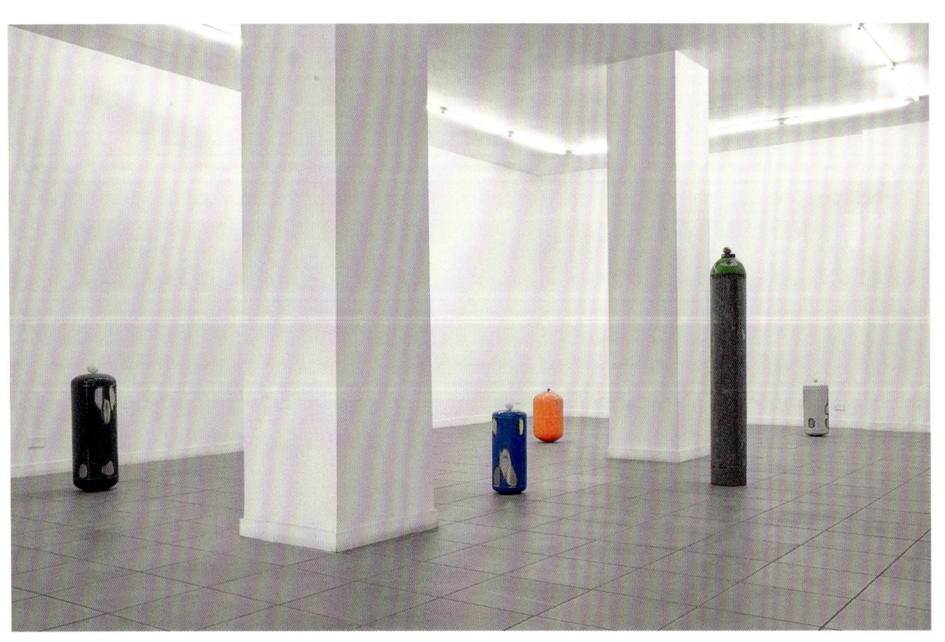

The Gallery Apart, Rom / Rome

2018

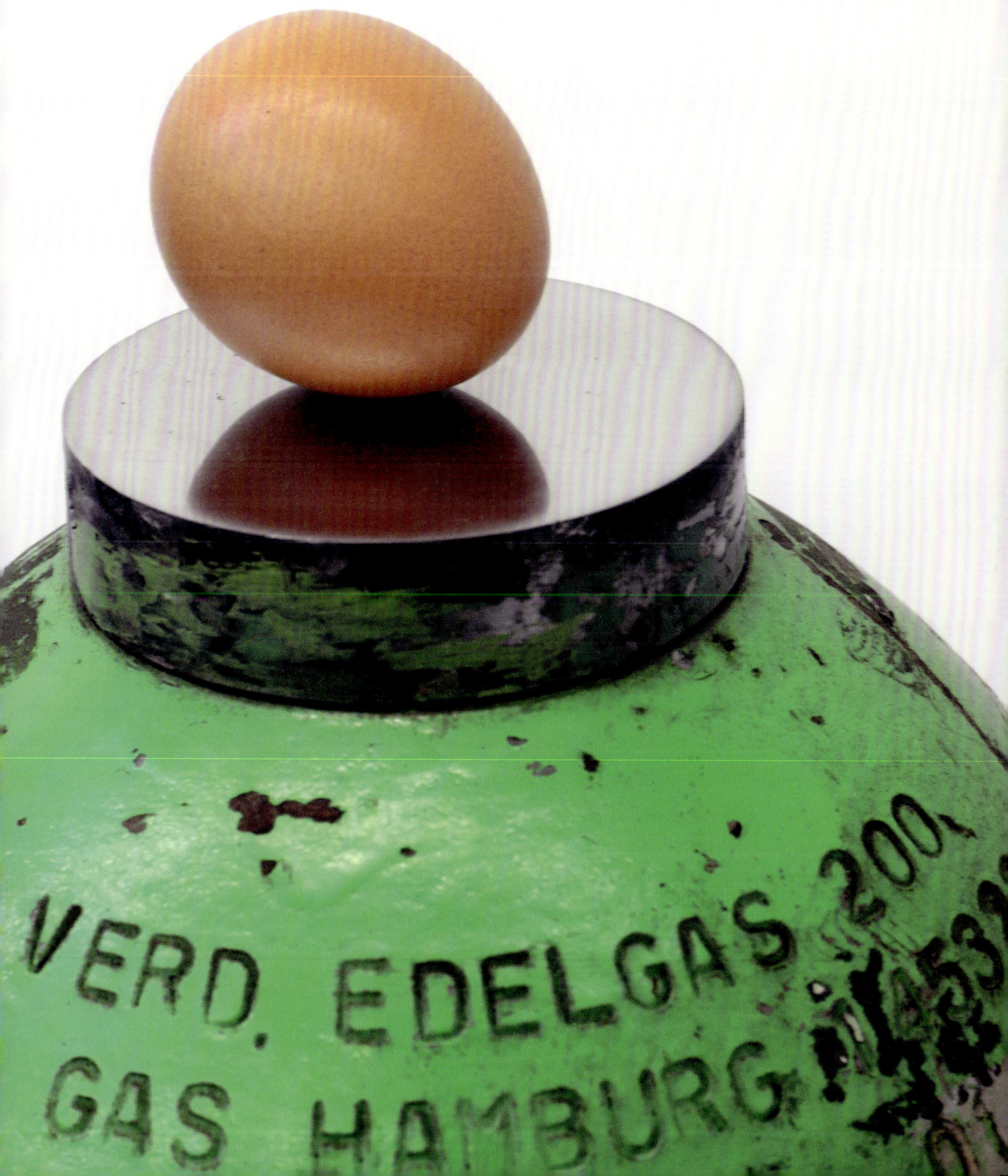
VERD. EDELGAS 200
GAS HAMBURG

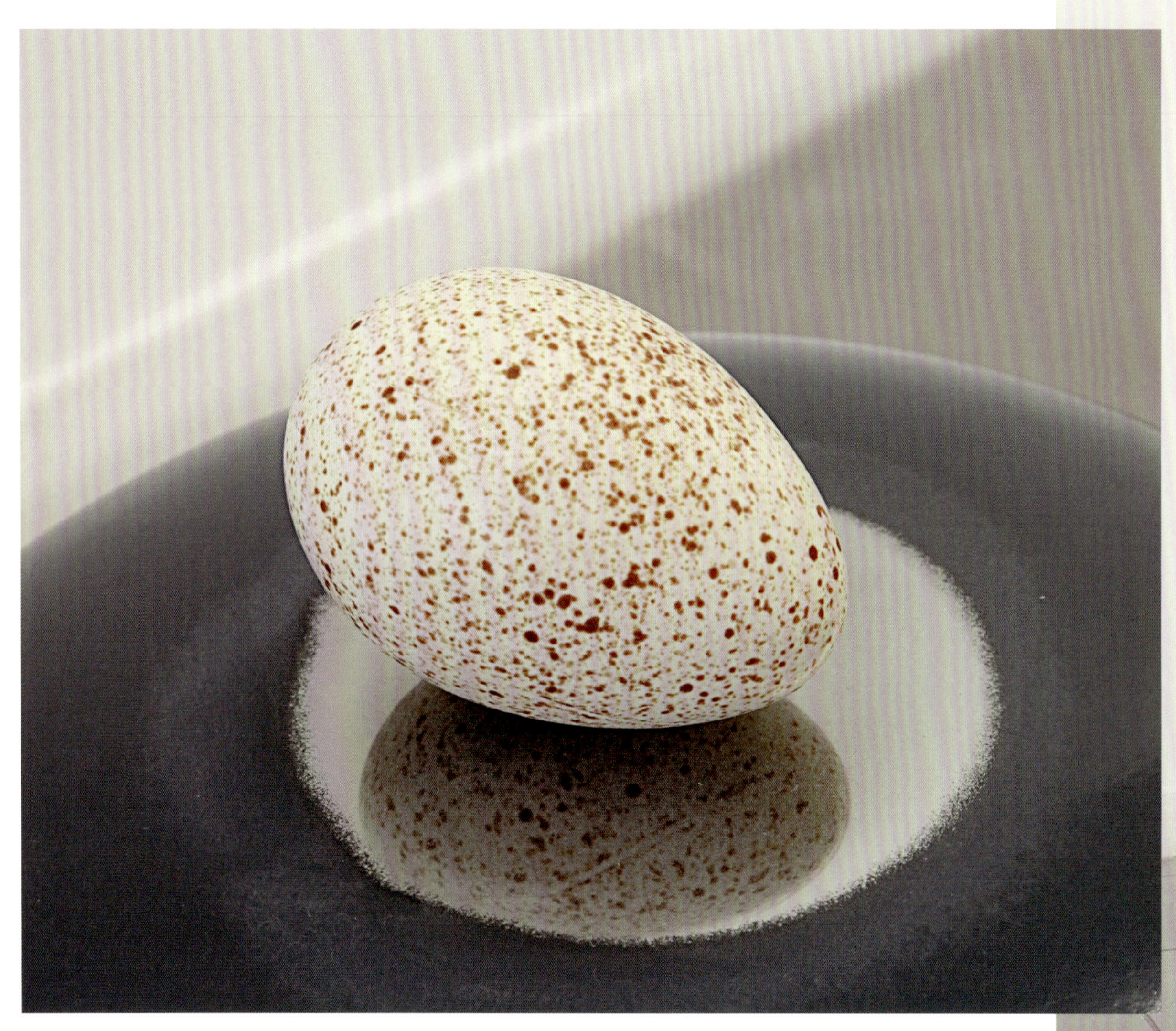

Sealed Vessels (2018)
Gasflaschen, Hühnereier /
gas bottles, chicken eggs

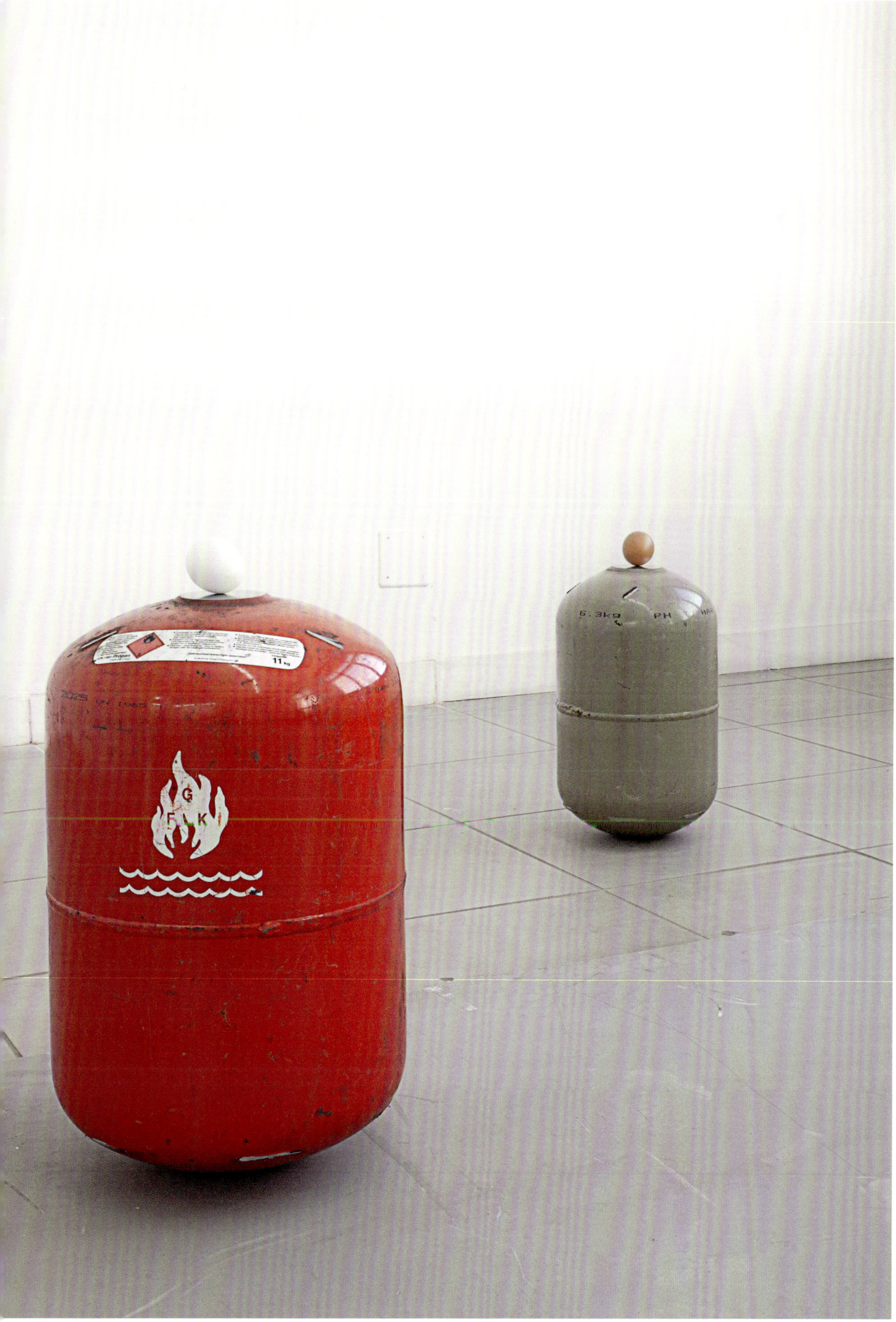

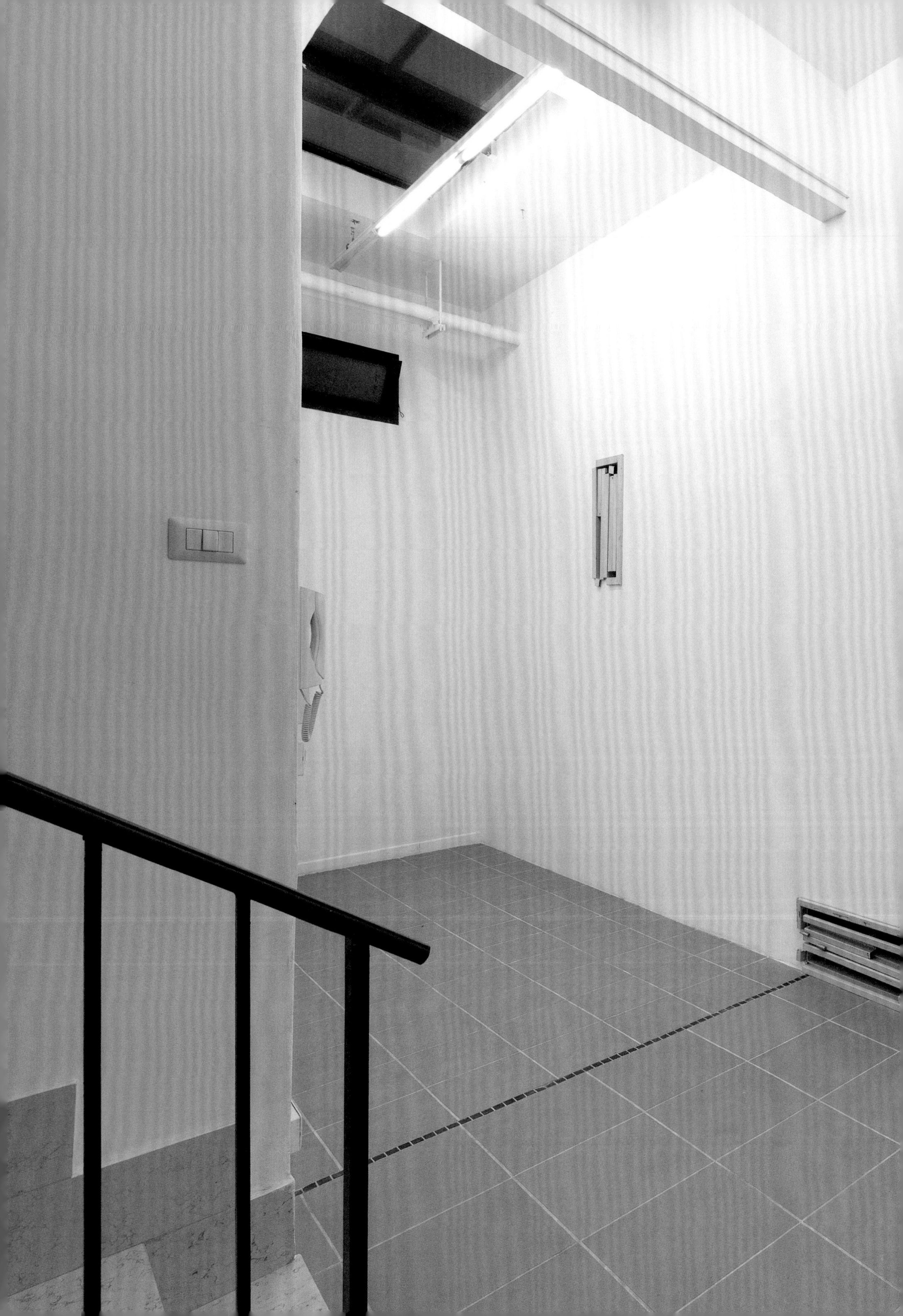

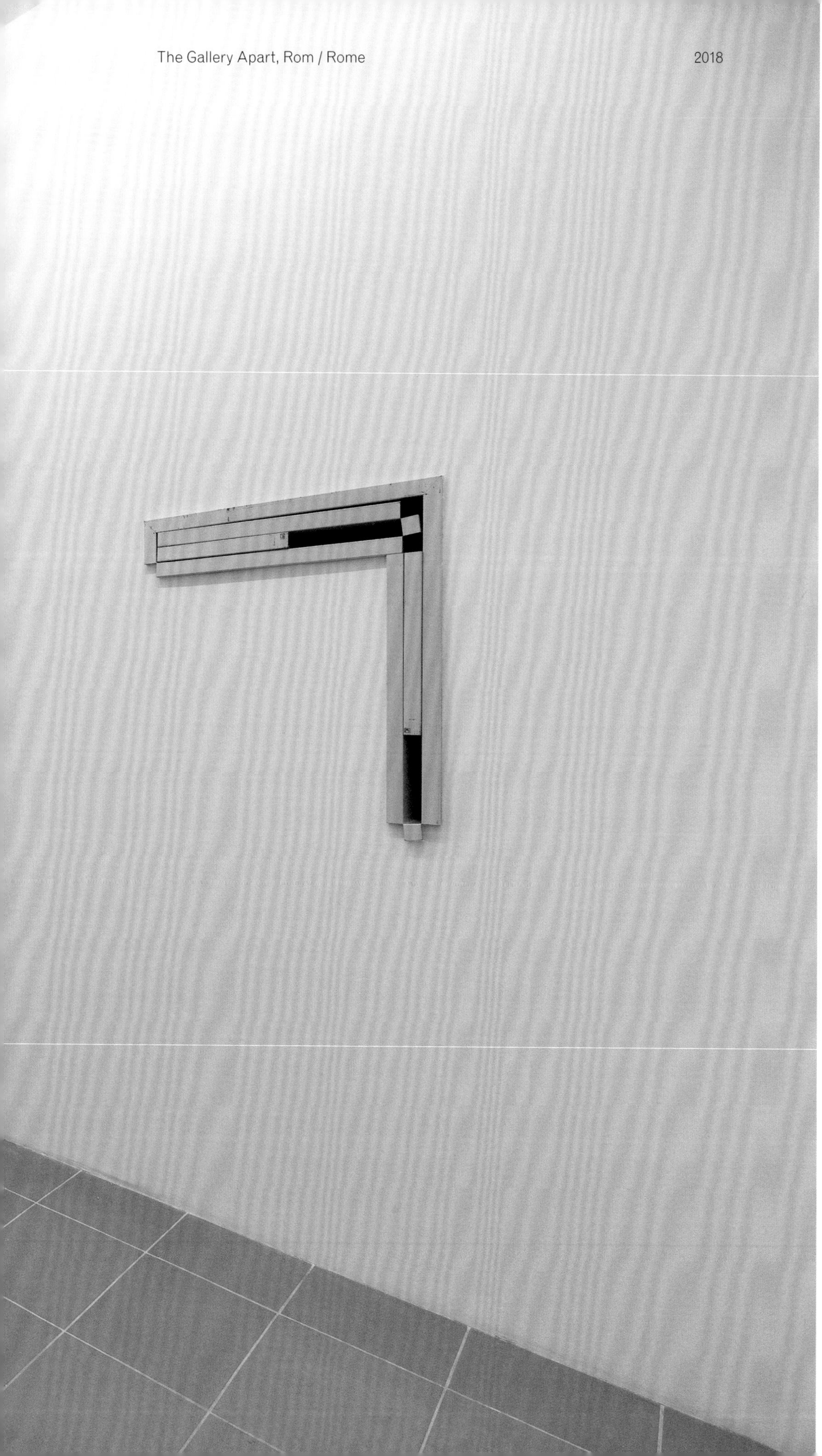

Rahmen / Frames (2018)
Türzargen, Gipskarton, Farbe /
doorframes, plasterboard, paint
400×680 cm

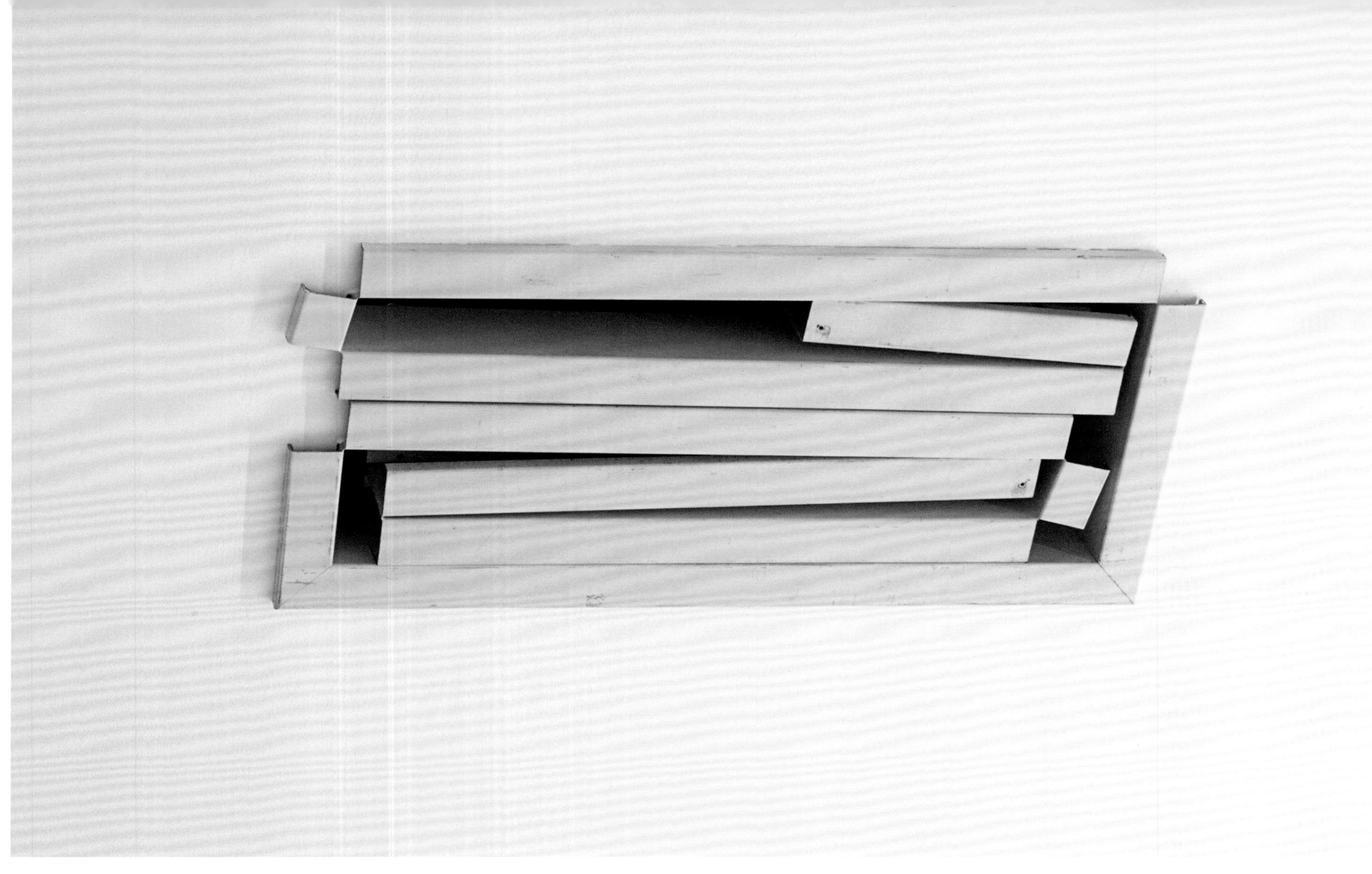

Rahmen / Frames (2018)
Türzarge, Gipskarton, Farbe /
doorframe, plasterboard, paint
80 × 34 × 15 cm

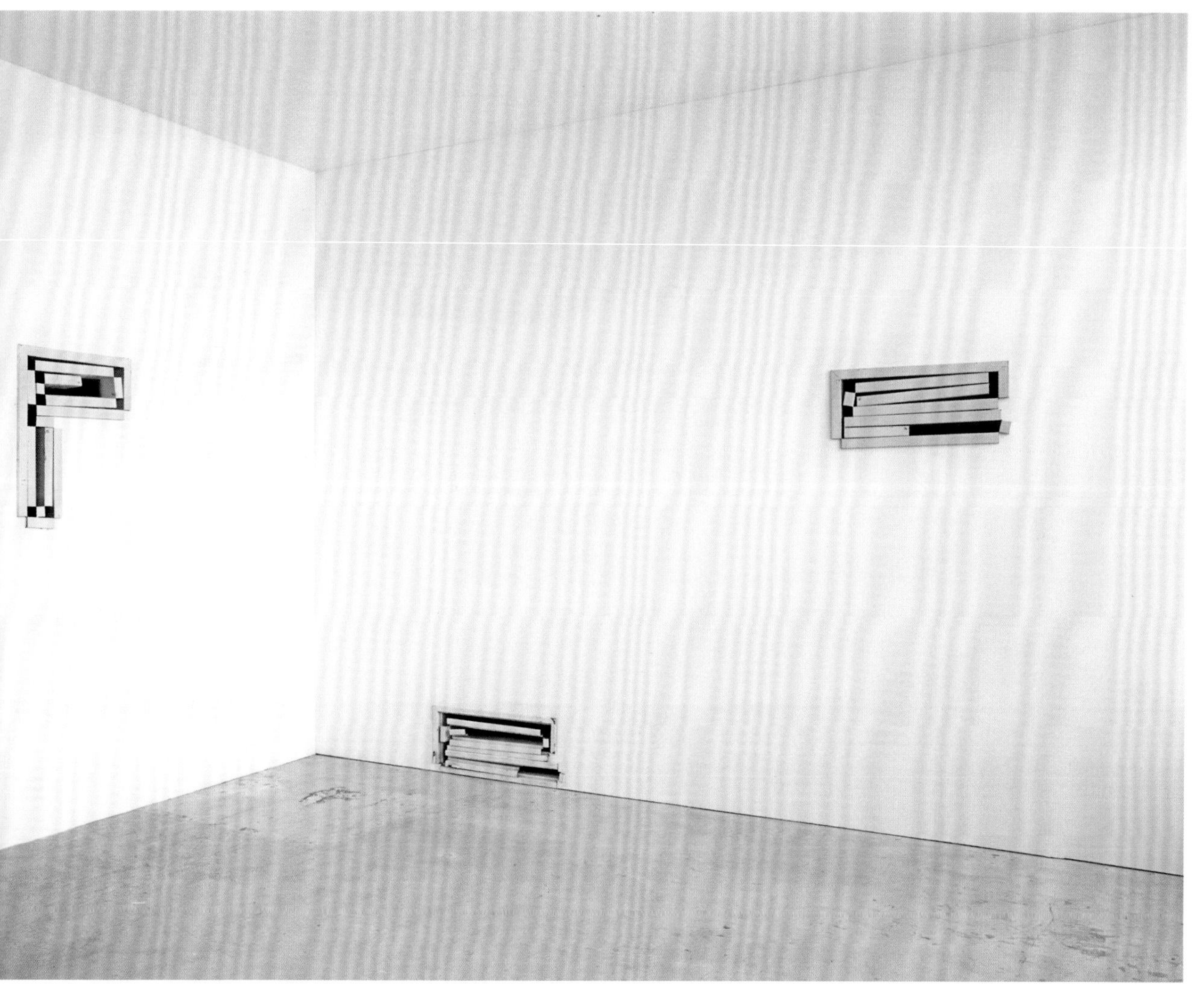

Rahmen / Frames (2018)
Türzargen, Spanplatte, Holz, Farbe / doorframes, chipboard, wood, paint

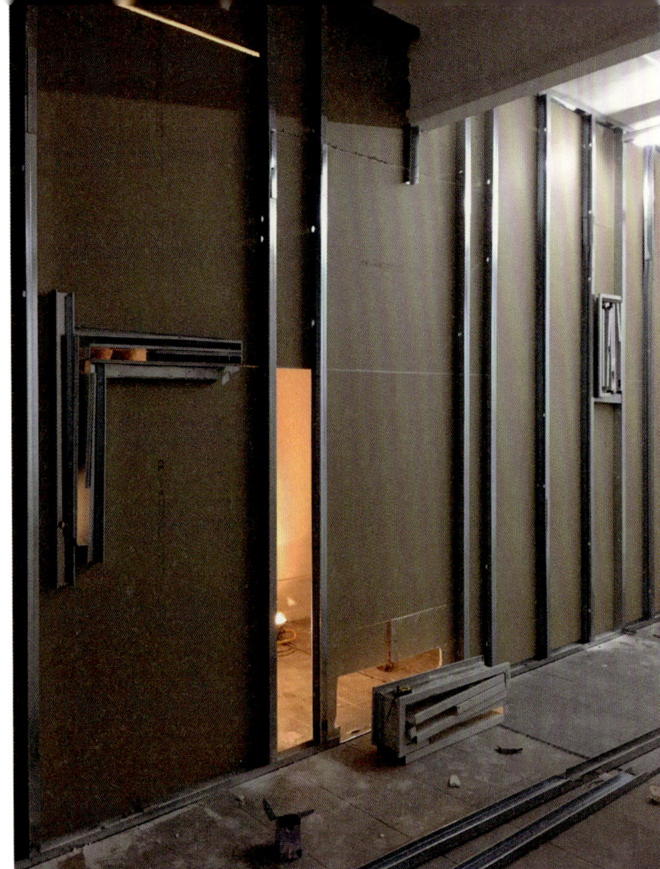

Aufbau von / installation of *Rahmen* / *Frames* (2018)

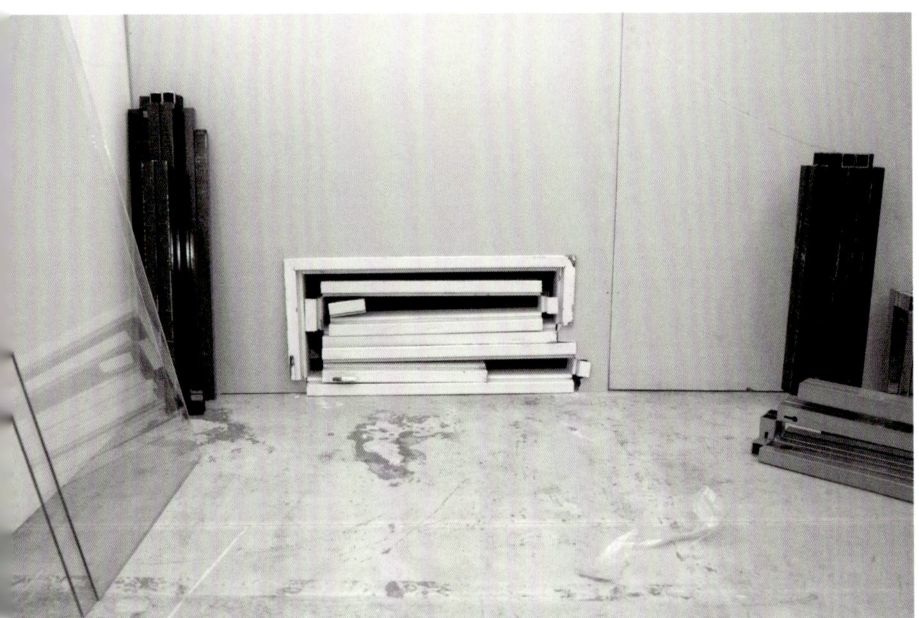

Atelierskizze *Rahmen* / studio sketch *Frames* (2018)

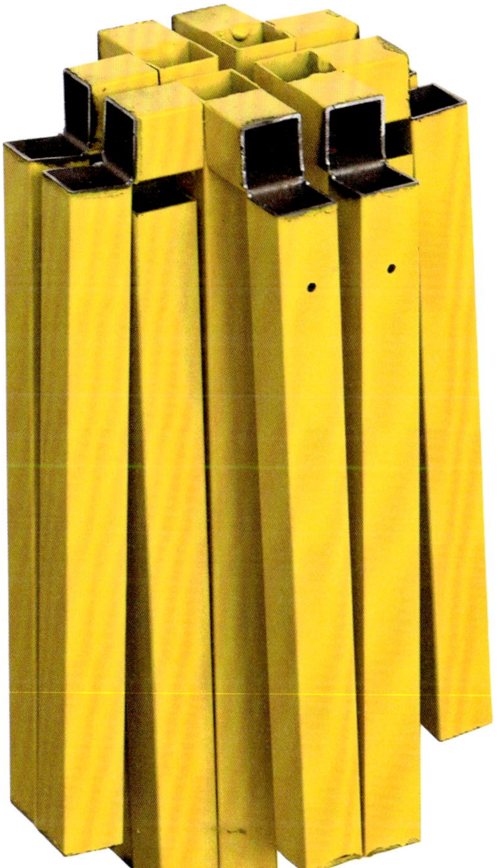

Selbstgespräche (gelb) / Soliloqui (yellow) (2016)
Tischgestell / table frame
45 × 21 × 21 cm

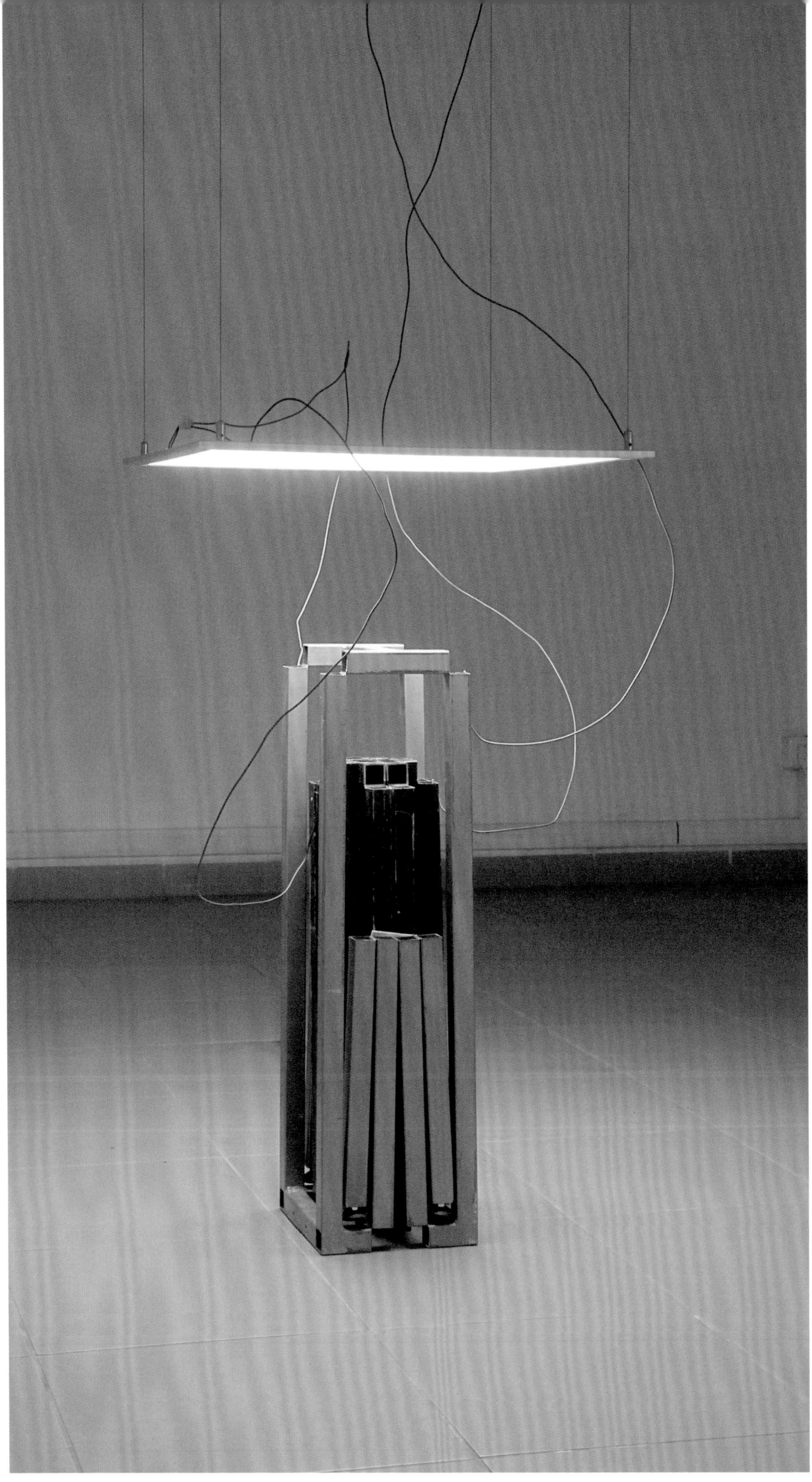

Stray Currents (2017)
Tischgestelle, LED-Panel mit Treiber, Kabel /
table frames, LED panel with driver, cable
91 × 24 × 26 cm

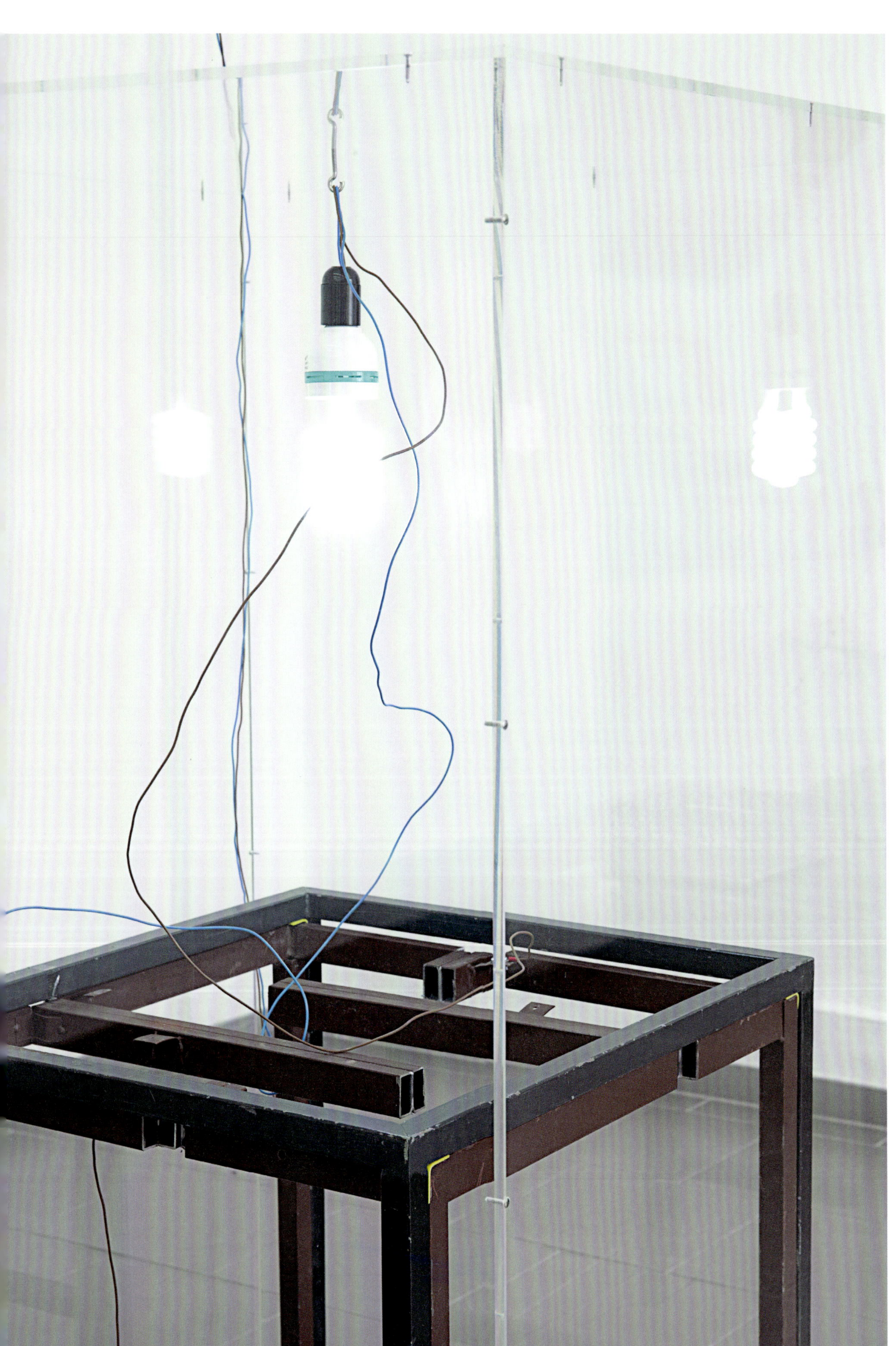

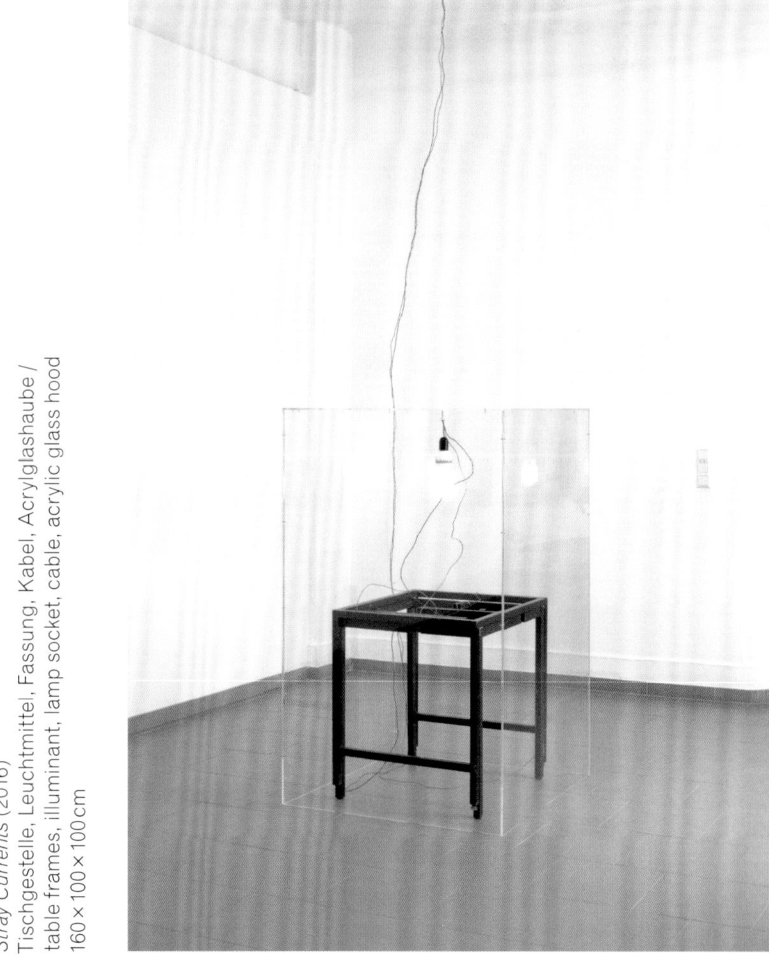

Stray Currents (2016)
Tischgestelle, Leuchtmittel, Fassung, Kabel, Acrylglashaube /
table frames, illuminant, lamp socket, cable, acrylic glass hood
160 × 100 × 100 cm

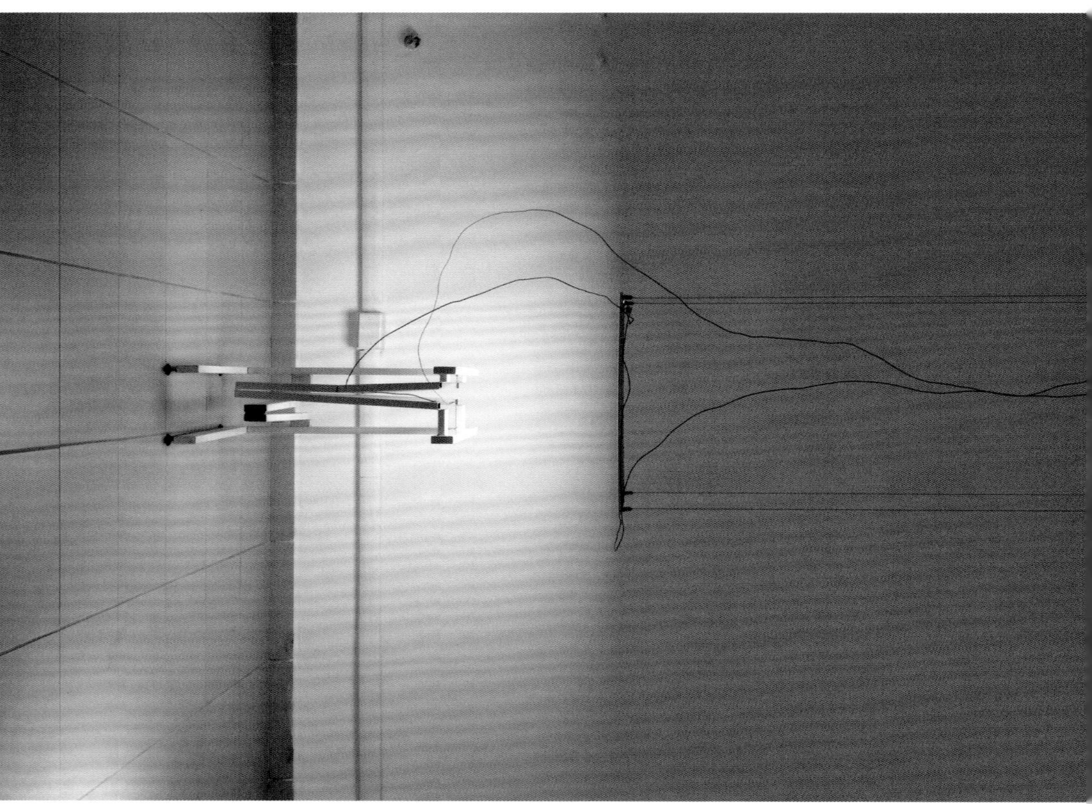

Stray Currents (2017)
Tischgestell, LED-Panel mit Treiber, Kabel / table frame, LED panel with driver, cable
76 × 21 × 60 cm

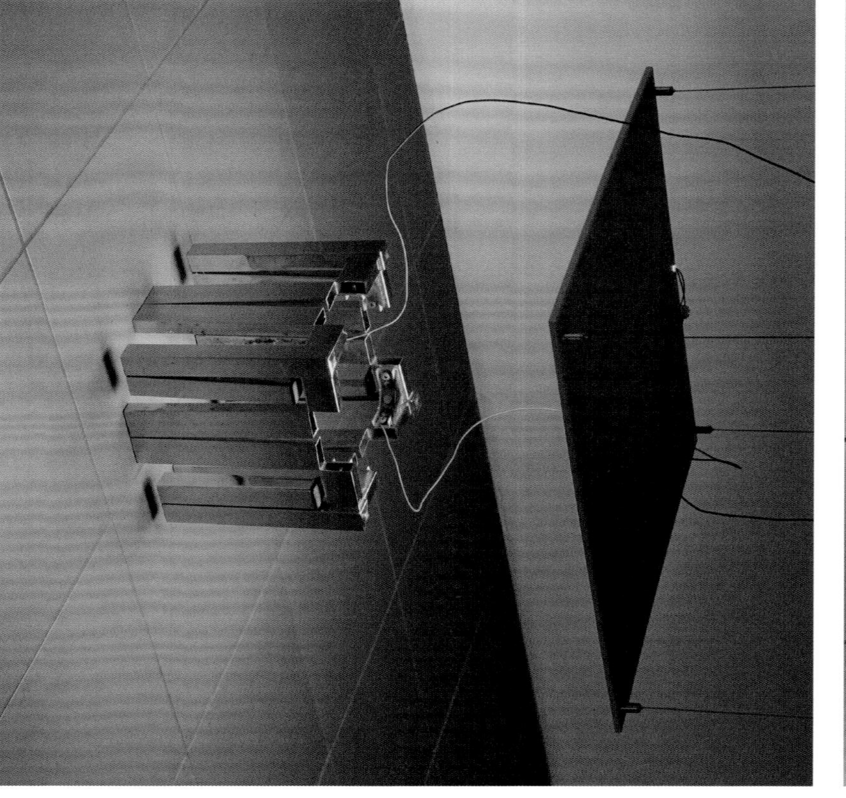

Stray Currents (2017)
Tischgestell, LED-Panel mit Treiber, Kabel / table frame, LED panel with driver, cable
24 × 24 × 24 cm

The Tendency to Look Up (2013)
Türzarge / doorframe
60 × 42 × 35 cm

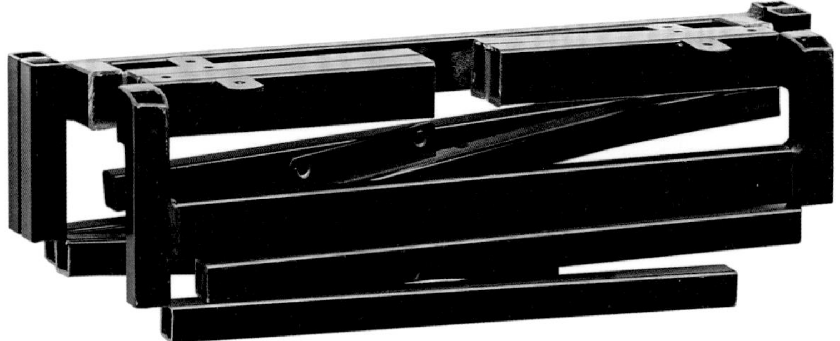

Sitzordnung / Seating Arrangement (2016)
Stuhlgestell / chair frame
14 × 47 × 14 cm

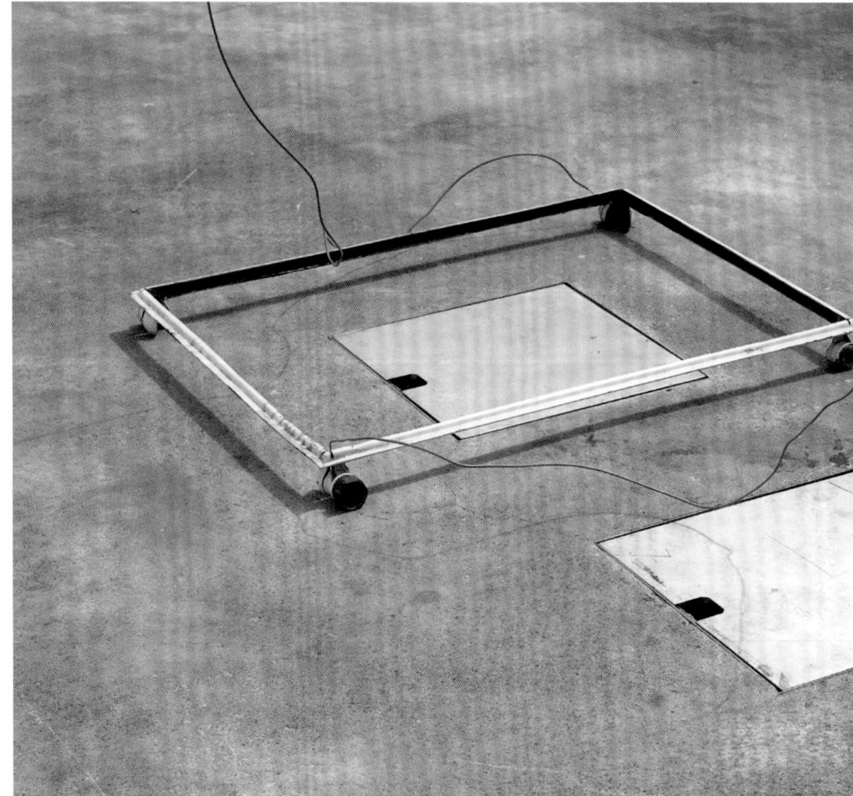

Stray Currents (2017)
Heizkörper, LED-Panel mit Treiber, Kabel /
heater, LED panel with driver, cable
5 × 63 × 52 cm

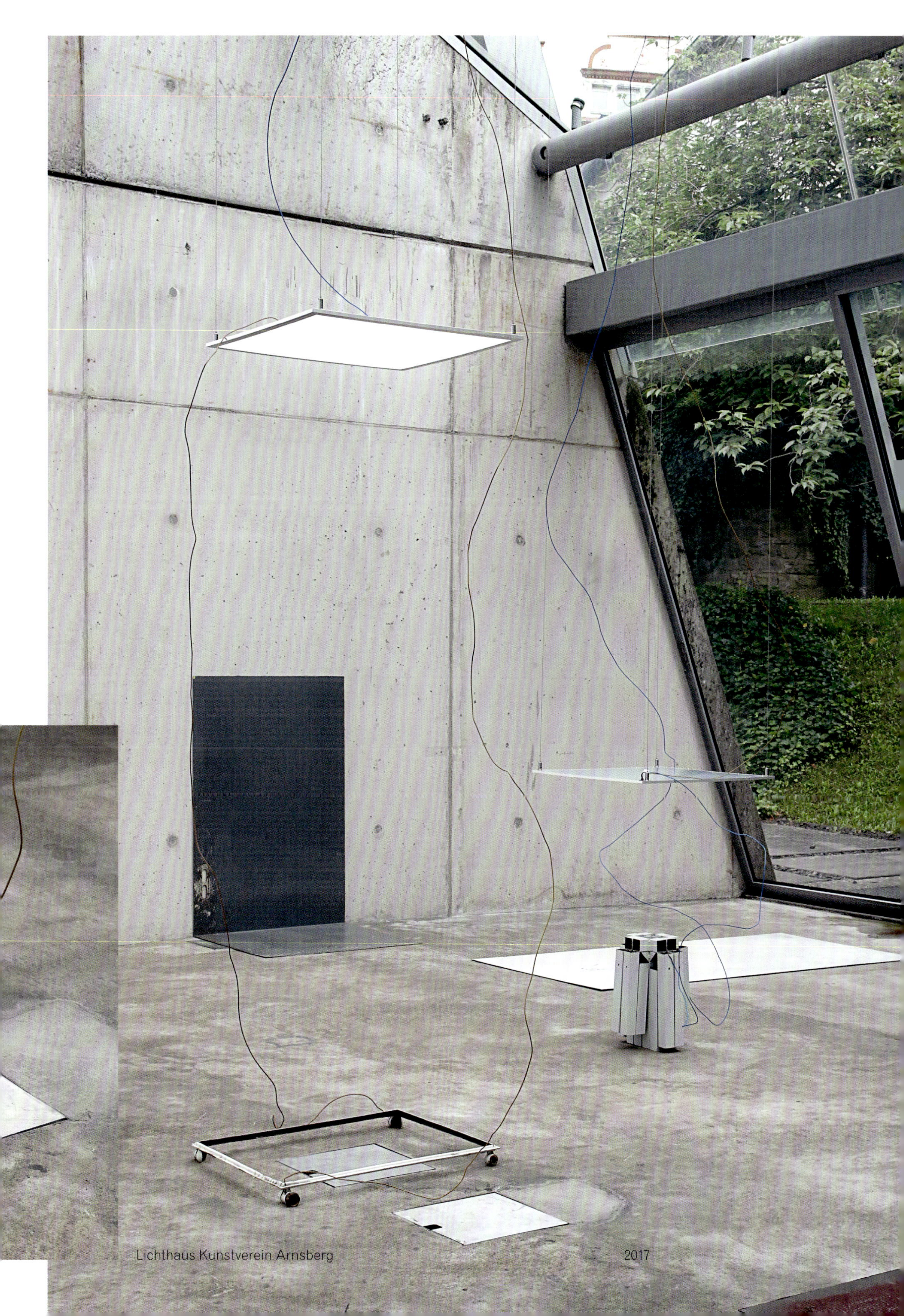

Lichthaus Kunstverein Arnsberg 2017

Stray Currents (2017)
Blechkiste, LED-Panel mit Treiber, Kabel /
metal box, LED panel with driver, cable
37 × 47 × 66 cm

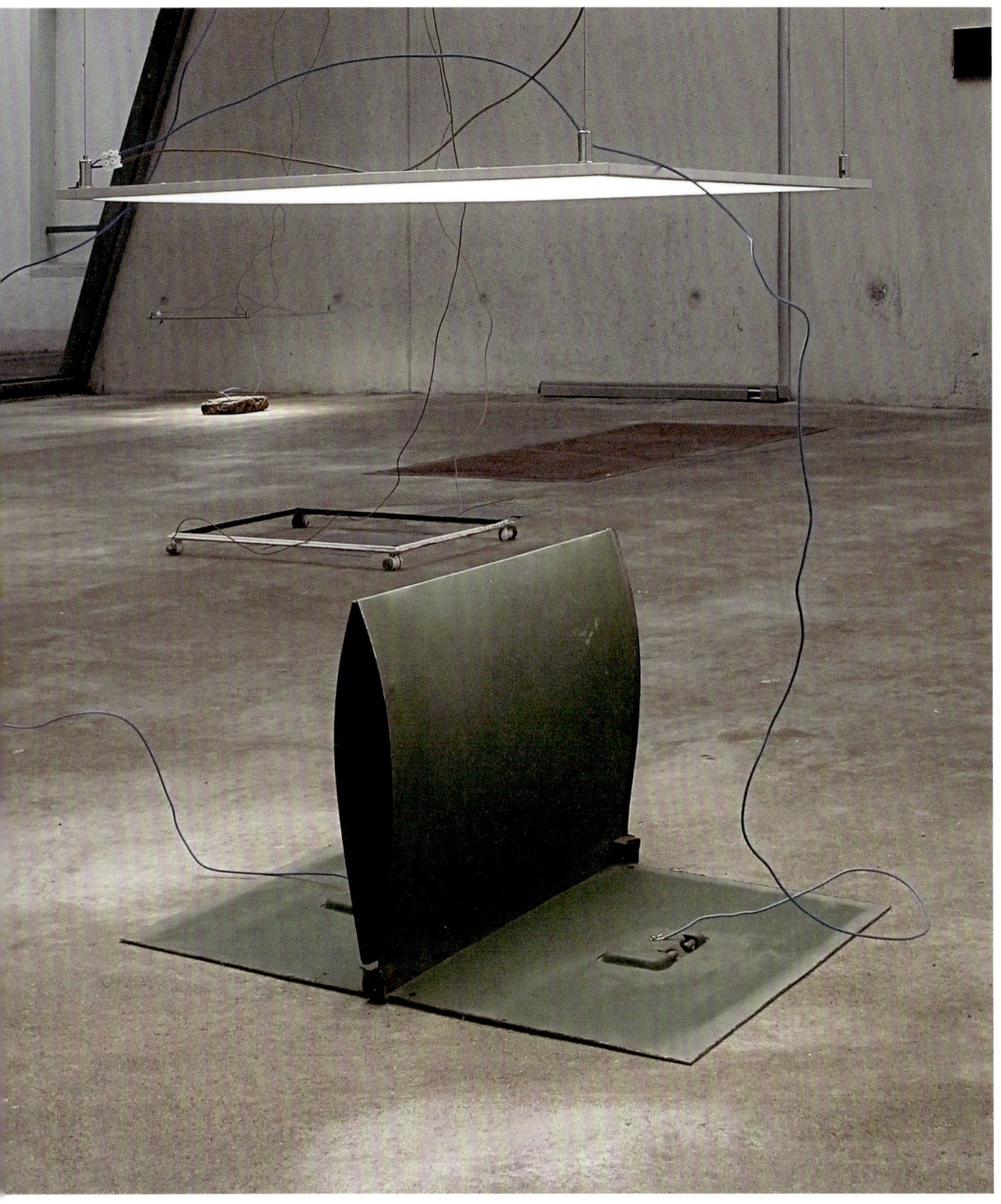

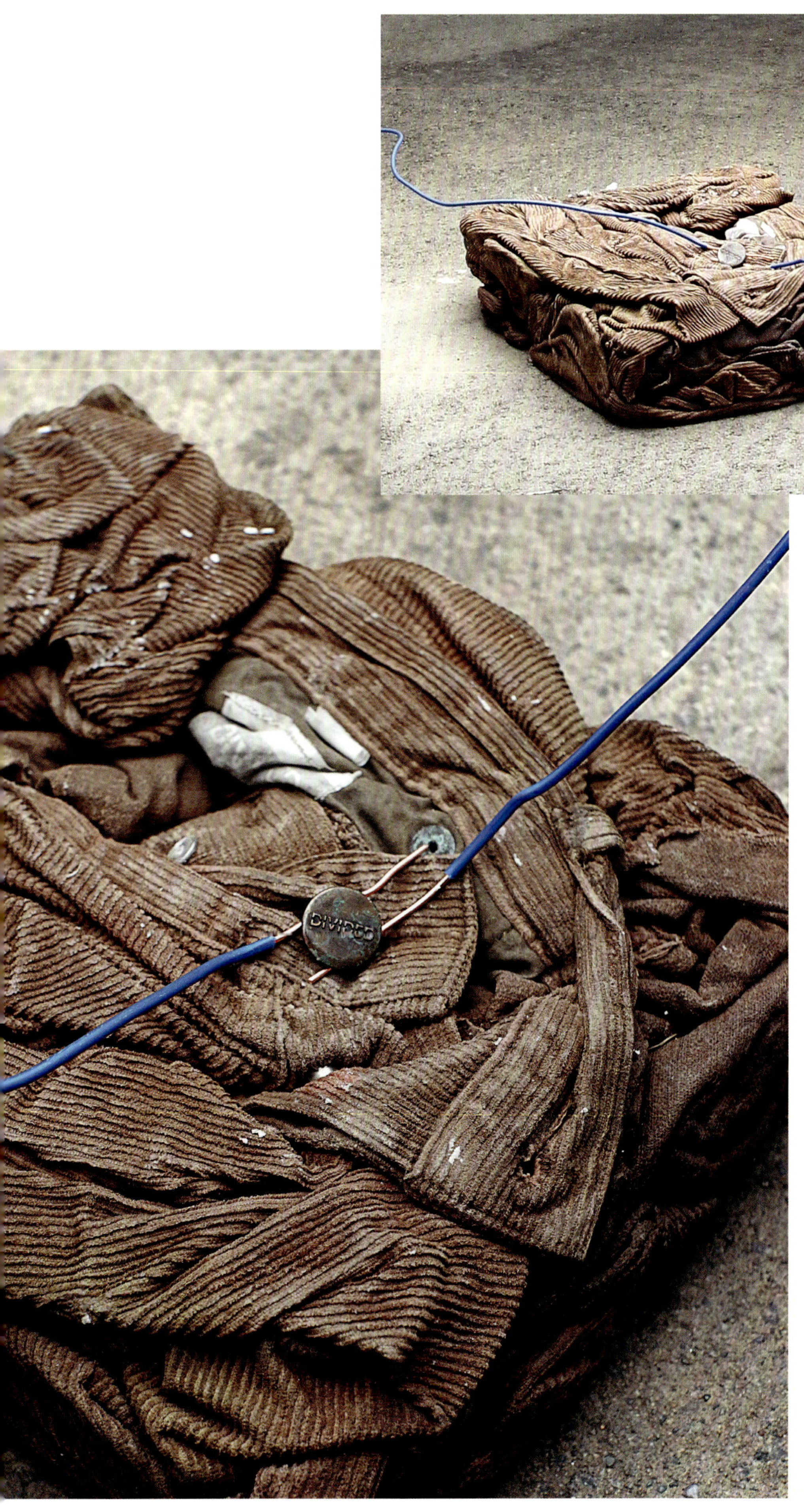

Stray Currents (2017)
Cordhose, LED-Panel mit Treiber, Kabel /
Corduroy trousers, LED panel with driver, cable
6×20×25cm

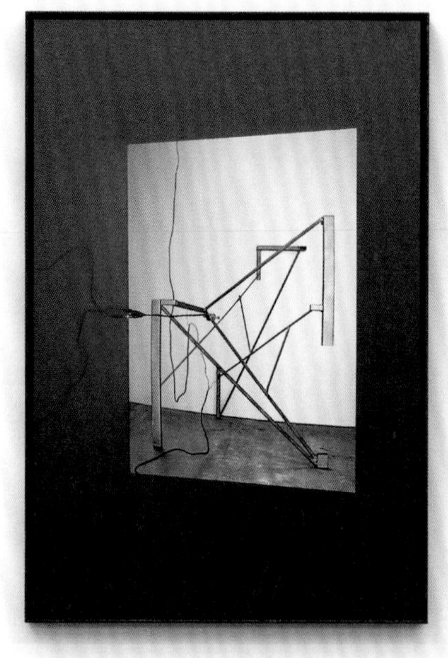

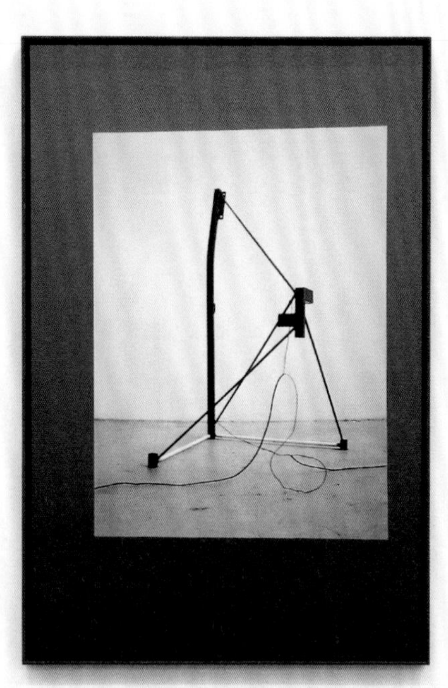

Live Wires (2017)
Inkjet Print, Alu-PE-Verbundplatte, Stahlrahmen /
inkjet print, Alu-Pe composite, steel frame
62 × 41,5 cm

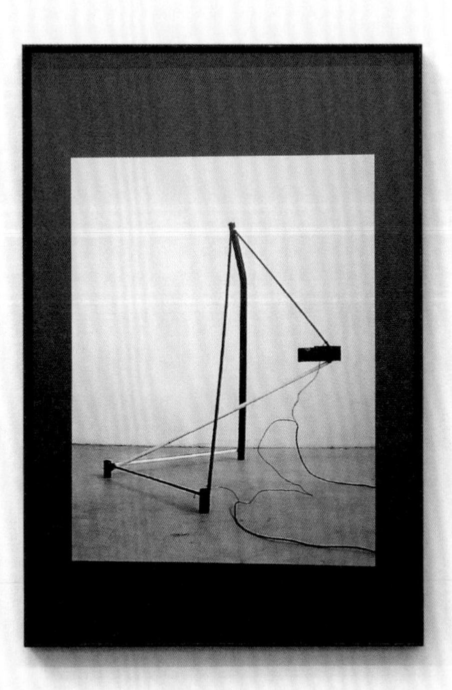

Live Wires (2017)
Stuhlgestelle, Stahl, Dämmplatten /
chair frames, steel, insulating boards

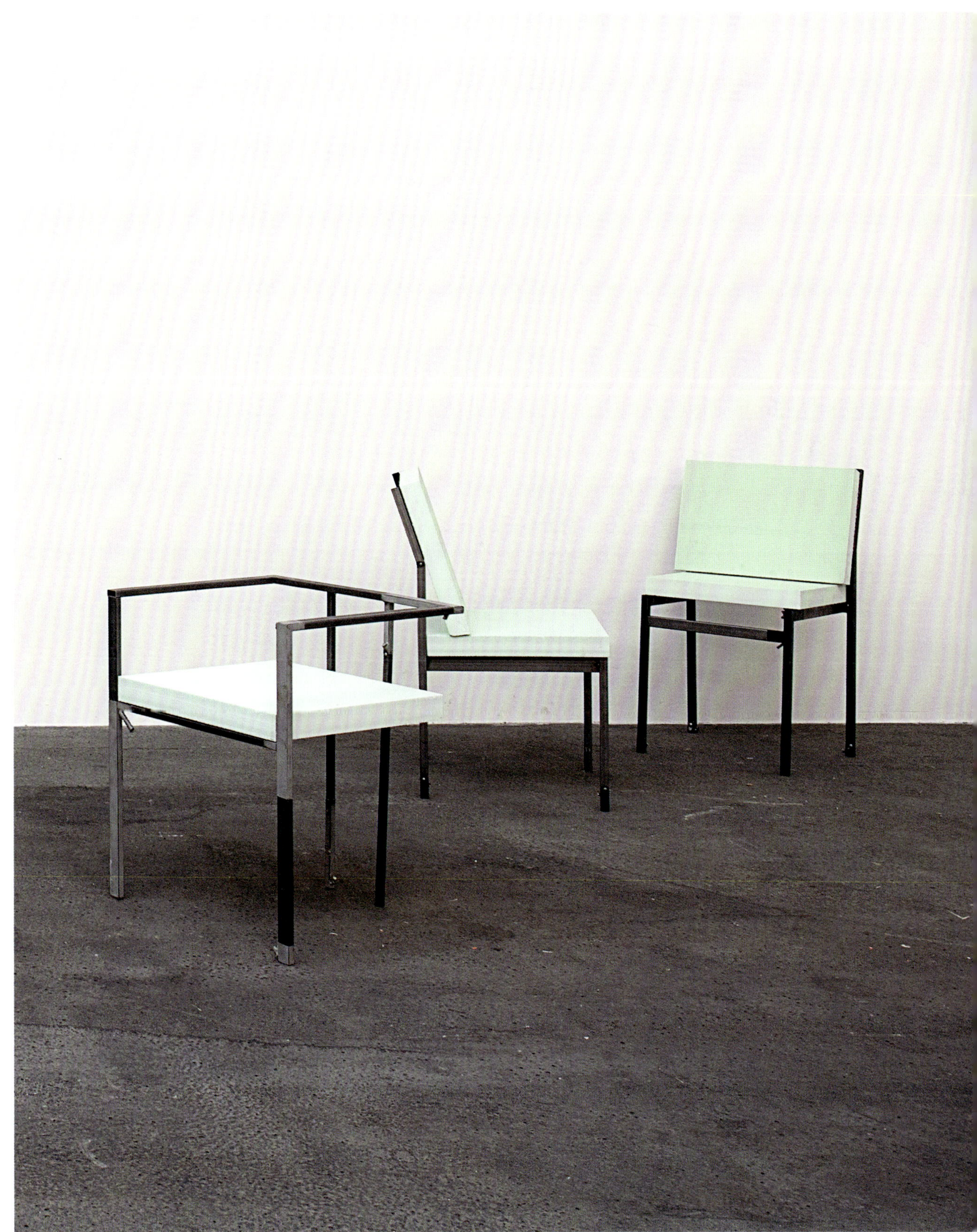

Über das Schweigen

Wer über Florian Neufeldts fallenstellende Kunstwerke schreiben will, ist gut beraten, die Kapitulationsurkunde gleich im ersten Absatz zu unterzeichnen. Denn seine Arbeiten setzen alles daran, sich einer beschreibenden und bewertenden Sprache zu entziehen. Sie umschließen sorgsam eine Leere, in die sich auch mit größter Anstrengung kein erklärendes Wort einfügen lässt. Sie sind geschlossene Sinnkreisläufe des skulpturalen Selbsterhalts. Die Kunst leistet in ihnen den paradoxen Aufwand, wahrnehmbar zu werden, ohne auf irgendetwas als sich selbst zu verweisen. Anders als in den Objekten der Minimal Art sollen sie dabei aber nicht durch Reduktion überwältigen. Mit der Stringenz physikalischer Versuchsaufbauten demonstrieren sie ihre Überflüssigkeit. Überdeutlich wie in einem Wachtraum machen sie klar, dass es hier nichts zu suchen und erst recht nichts anderes zu finden gibt als die Sinnfälligkeit einer einfachen mathematischen Gleichung. T1 entspricht T2. Was links vom Gleichheitszeichen steht, erfüllt sich auch rechts. Wer einen Türrahmen zerlegt, verringert seine Länge. Gefaltet kann die Türzarge also einen kleineren Wandausschnitt füllen als den Durchgang zwischen zwei Räumen. Daraus lassen sich aber keine Aussagen über das Wesen von Türen treffen. Neufeldts Werk entzieht uns die Hoffnung, dass künstlerische Gleichungen uns die Welt erklären könnten. Sie entblößen die Sinnsuche in einem Tischgestell als Kinderglauben. Kunst ist keine Offenbarung. Sie steht unter dem begründeten Verdacht, ein Nullsummenspiel zu sein. Die Operatoren der Gleichung sind wichtig. Wer sich auf diese konzentriert, befreit sich von dem Vorurteil, durch die Betrachtung von Kunstwerken anstrengungslos die Welt zu verstehen. Ein Tischbein ist ein Tischbein und, anders als die Surrealisten glaubten, selbst eine Pfeife ist eine Pfeife. Wer wie die Kunsthistoriker in einem Tischbein Geister sieht, weil ein

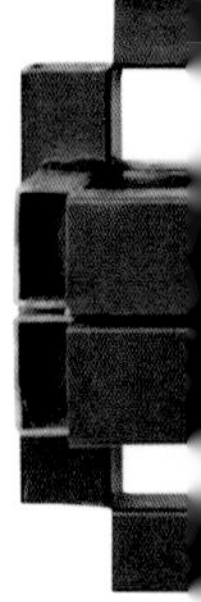

Tischordnung / Table Arrangement (2016)
Tischgestell / table frame
22 × 80 × 9 cm

On Silence

Anyone who wants to write about Florian Neufeldt's trap-setting works of art would be well advised to sign a surrender agreement within the first paragraph. For his works do everything in their power to elude descriptive and evaluative language. They studiously encompass a void that altogether defies the insertion of explanatory words, no matter how great the effort. They are closed significatory circuits of sculptural self-preservation. Within them art achieves the paradoxical complexity of being perceptible without referring to something other than itself. In contrast to Minimal Art objects, however, they do not set out to overwhelm us by means of reduction. Rather, they demonstrate their redundancy with all the rigour of a physics experiment. As blatantly as in a lucid dream, they reveal that there is nothing to seek and most certainly nothing to find within them beyond the scope of a simple mathematical equation. t_1 equals t_2. Whatever stands on the left of the equals sign is fulfilled on its right. If you dismantle a doorframe, say, you necessarily reduce its height. Once folded, the doorframe can fit into a wall opening smaller than the standard passage between two rooms. Yet this tells us little about the nature of doors per se. Neufeldt's work divests us of the hope that artistic equations might explain to us the world. Instead, they expose the naivety of looking for meaning in a table frame. Art is not a revelation. Indeed, there are reasonable grounds to suspect it might be a zero-sum game. What remain important are the operators in the equation. If we focus our attention on these, we liberate ourselves from the presupposition that the apprehension of works of art might somehow offer us easy access to understanding the world at large. A table leg is a table leg as, unlike the Surrealists believed, even a pipe is a pipe. Anyone, like an

Künstler es auf den Kopf gestellt hat, ist eben ein Geisterseher. Das ganze neufeldtsche Werk ist Gegenaufklärung gegen eine solch unlautere Beschäftigung. Sagen kann man nur, was man sieht. Der Interpret ist immer schon ein Narr. Die Grube, die den Narren hier gegraben wird, ist tief.

Damit wird das Augenmerk auf die Operatoren der Gleichungen Neufeldts gelegt. Wo so wenig zu finden ist, stellt sich die Frage, was man eigentlich sucht, schärfer als sonst. Es ist angesichts der offensichtlichen Nutzlosigkeit weiterer Analysen geradezu unvermeidlich, die eigene Sinnsuche zu hinterfragen. Neufeldt-Betrachter werden gleichermaßen genötigt und durch Witz verführt, genau jene unbehagliche Stelle einzunehmen, an der man sich einerseits noch nicht damit zufrieden gibt, das Objekt als bloßes Ding zur Kenntnis zu nehmen wie Marcel Duchamps notorisches Urinal (*Fountain*, 1917), ein umgewidmetes Fundstück, das seine Macht allein aus der Gnade der Institution bezieht, die es dem Publikum darbietet, das allenfalls über den Künstler als Marionetten- und Schachspieler spekulieren kann, an der Keramik des Toilettenbeckens aber keine Erkenntnisse abzulesen vermag. Das Ding erklärt sich bei Neufeldt zur Kunst. Es beruht auf präzisen Entscheidungen seines Schöpfers. Andererseits aber ist es durchsichtig

art historian, who sees ghosts in a table leg merely because an artist has placed it upside down is seeing ghosts and no more than that. Neufeldt's entire oeuvre works to counter such a dubious occupation. We can only speak of what we see. The interpreter is always already a fool. The pit that is dug here for fools is deep.

Let us turn our attention, then, to the operators in Neufeldt's equations. Where so little is to be found, the question of what one might actually be seeking becomes all the more pertinent. Given the obvious futility of further analysis, we inevitably begin to question our own search for meaning. As viewers of Neufeldt's works we are equally coerced and seduced by the wit of the latter to adopt precisely that uncomfortable position in which, on the one hand, we are not content to acknowledge the object as a mere thing, as in the case of Marcel Duchamp's notorious urinal (*Fountain*, 1917), a repurposed found object that derives its power solely by the grace of the institution

wie ein Fensterglas und gibt jede weitergehende Spekulation über seinen Gehalt dem spöttischen Gelächter preis. Eine Türzarge ist eine Türzarge und als Ornament an einer Wand zusätzlich eine Ornament gewordene Türzarge. Kluge Idee, sie so in einen Hohlraum zu versenken, dass sie wie ein dreidimensionales Stück Malerei die klassisch gewordene Debatte über Flachheit und Objekthaftigkeit eines Gemäldes auf den Kopf stellt und die grafische Qualität des kleinen Gelasses in der Ausstellungswand wie einen Zaubertrick präsentiert. Die Gleichung aber bleibt gleich. Der Zaubertrick ist durchschaubar. Niemals scheint Neufeldt der Versuchung zu erliegen, den Trick zu verhüllen, die Rechnung zu verkomplizieren oder die Geste zur Geschichte auszubauen. Bevor das zu Grabe getragene Narrativ seinen untoten Kopf aus dem Grab strecken kann, hat der Künstler seinen Prozess längst abgeschlossen. 2+2=4. Wer will da den Meister wegen seiner Rechenkunst preisen oder in der Addition den Weltgeist wiedererkennen? Tatsächlich werden hier nicht nur die Kunsthistoriker wortkarg, sondern auch die vielen zu allem entschlossenen Kunstbewunderer. Was bleibt ihnen? So etwas wie der Widerhall, das körperliche Vibrato,

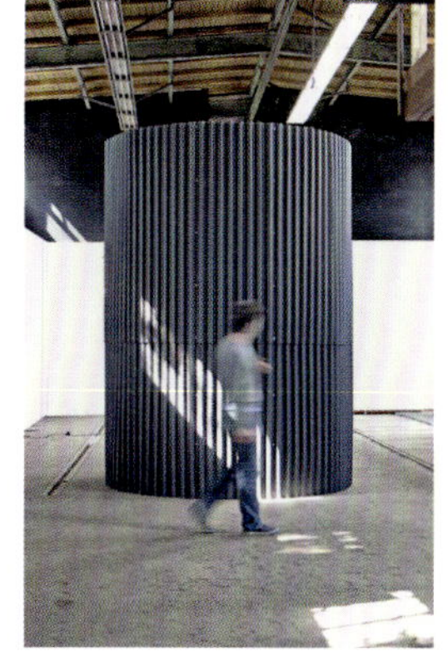

Come and Go (2008)
Bitumenplatten, Holz, Motor, Steuerung / bituminised board, wood, motor, control unit
340 × 270 × 270 cm

that presents it to an audience at best able to speculate about the artist as a puppeteer or chess player and unlikely to garner any knowledge from the ceramic of the toilet bowl. In Neufeldt's work, the thing declares itself to be art, resting upon the precise decisions made by its creator. On the other hand, however, the thing is as transparent as window glass, thus making a mockery of any further speculation as to its content. A doorframe is a doorframe, while as an ornament on a wall, it is a doorframe that has also become an ornament. It's a clever idea to recess it into a wall in such a way as to resemble a piece of three-dimensional painting, thereby both subverting the traditional debate about the flatness and objecthood of a painting and presenting the graphical quality of the small chamber in the exhibition wall as a magic trick. Even so, the equation remains the same. The magic trick is easy to see through. Yet Neufeldt never seems to succumb to the temptation of concealing the trick, of complicating the calculation or

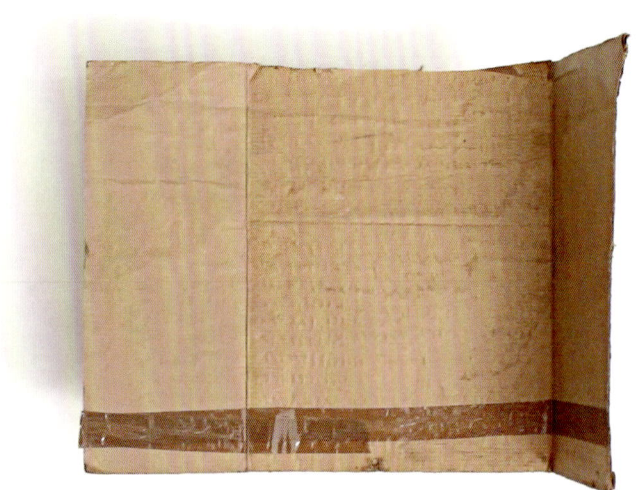

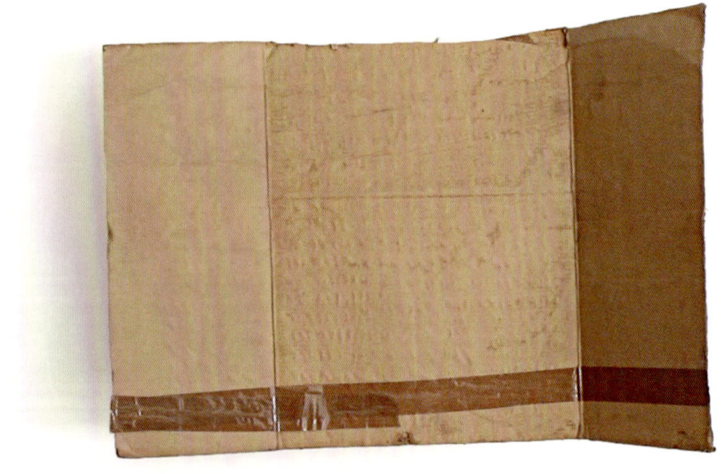

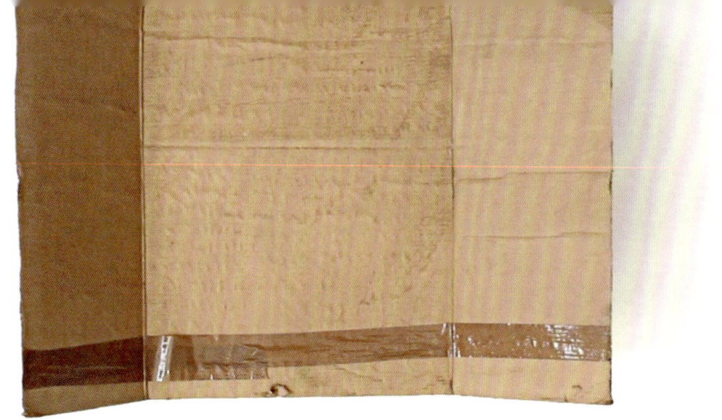

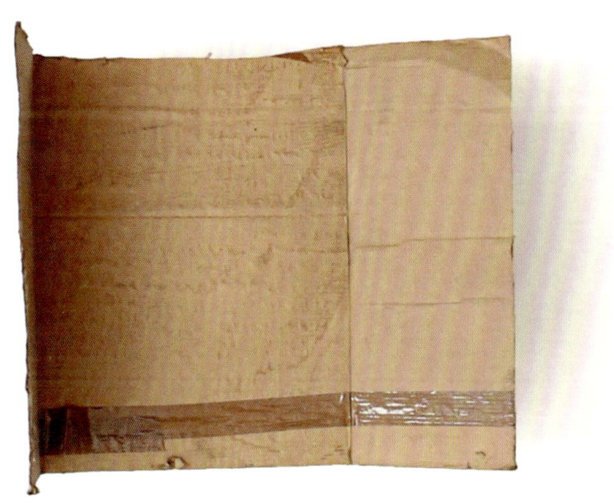

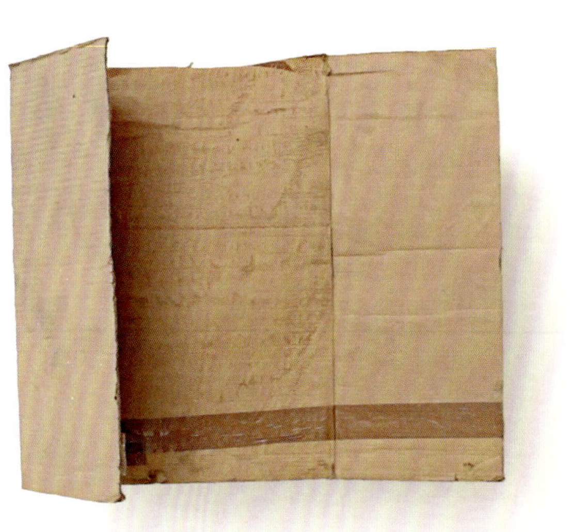

Kopernikanischer Karton / Copernican Carboard (2009)
Videoprojektion / video projection
16:9 (Loop / loop), 6:32 min

die Schwingung im Raum, wenn der Pianist seinen Schlüssel in den Konzertflügel wirft?
Wer Duchamp verehrt, bewundert ein Axiom und gleich darauf die eigene Fähigkeit, es zu begreifen. Wer von Neufeldt in die irritierende Lage gebracht wird, umkonfigurierte Bauteile, ihrer Zwecke entkleidete Inventarreste, selbstbezügliche Stromkreise oder mit dem eigenen Systemerhalt beschäftigte Mechaniken zu beobachten, sieht einem Künstler bei der Arbeit zu, der seine Gleichungen mit der Effizienz und Klarheit eines japanischen Kalligrafen präsentiert. Wie viele Faltungen bedingen hinreichend, dass ein Objekt zur Gleichung wird? Welche Zusatzleistung macht aus der Manipulation einer Wand einen immerhin lesbaren Prozess? Ab wann hat eine mechanisch angetriebene Bewegung Anspruch auf unsere Aufmerksamkeit? Da sich über das, was geschieht, nie etwas ohne Übereifer auf der Seite der Beobachter sagen lässt; da der Aufwand jeder Äußerung redundanter und willkürlicher als der Beobachtungsgegenstand ist, stehen sich in jeder Installation Florian Neufeldts zwei ungleiche Spieler gegenüber. Wer sich bewegt, verliert. Wer etwas sucht, fällt

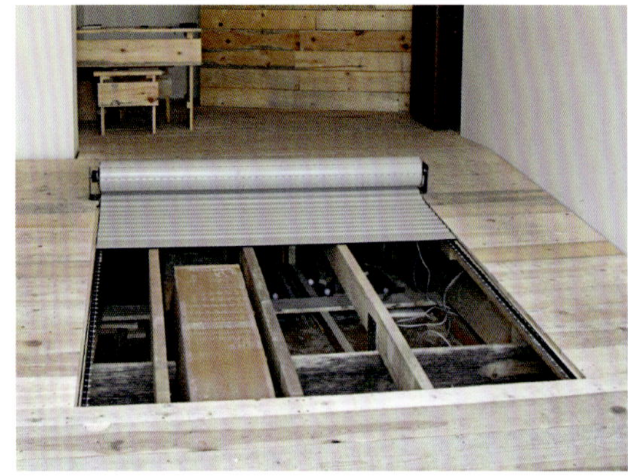

developing the gesture into a story. Before the buried narrative can rear its undead head out of the grave, the artist has long since completed his process. 2+2=4. Who would want to commend the master for his arithmetic or recognise the world spirit in the summation? In fact, art historians are not the only ones to respond with reticence here but also the many art aficionados typically up for anything. With what are they left? Something akin to the reverberation, the corporeal vibrato, the sound waves we would hear if a pianist were to throw his or her keys into a grand piano?
Those who esteem Duchamp admire an axiom and a moment later their own ability to understand it. Those who are led by Neufeldt into the confusing situation of observing reconfigured components – odds and ends of fixtures divested of their purpose, self-referential electrical circuits or mechanisms dealing with the preservation of their own system – find themselves watching an artist at work who presents

in die Grube. Wer spricht, verfälscht die Gleichung. Man kann, das ist das eigentliche mechanische Geheimnis dieser Kunst, vor jenen Objekten nur lachen. Nicht weil sie notwendig komisch wären, sondern weil sie in ihrer Pointierung Witzen gleichen, ohne Witze zu sein. Der Lachende begreift im Nu und erkennt die Unmöglichkeit, eine Pointe zu analysieren und zu kommentieren. Der Reflex schlägt die Reflexion. Die Beobachtung des Beobachtungsprozesses drängt sich in den Raum. Der Boden wird schwankend. Besteht der Genuss in diesem Spiel allein in unserer Freiheit zur Mitarbeit? Verführt uns der Umstand, dass es so wenig Verpflichtung gibt, einem am Boden montierten Rollladen zu applaudieren, weil er uns vorübergehend unter die Dielen blicken lässt, dazu, dass wir ohne jede Einschränkung mit der Leere einen Pakt schließen können, der uns weit mehr Raum lässt und weit mehr zumutet als ein in seiner Theatralik minimalistischer Würfel? Sind Neufeldts Gleichungen eher Appelle an unsere Selbsterkenntnis oder Ausbeutung unserer Übermotivation bei der Sinnproduktion? Sind sie Spiegel unserer zirkulären Gedanken oder Fluchtwege daraus, weil sich in ihnen ohnehin alles denken lässt, da eine Gleichung ja über nichts etwas sagt als das, was sich links oder rechts des Gleichheitszeichens befindet?

Laden (2008)
Rollladen, Motor, Steuerung /
shutter, motor, control
30 × 180 × 200 cm

his equations with the efficiency and clarity of a Japanese calligrapher. How many folds does it take to turn an object into an equation? What else is required to make the manipulation of a wall into a process that is at least legible? At what point does a mechanically driven movement deserve our attention? In so far as nothing can ever be said about what is happening without the viewer becoming over-zealous, in so far as the effort involved in every utterance about the object is more redundant and arbitrary than the object itself, Florian Neufeldt's installations invariably pit two unequal players against one another. Whoever moves, loses. Whoever searches for something, falls into the pit. Whoever speaks, falsifies the equation. In the face of such objects, we can only laugh – that is the real mechanical secret of this art. Not because the objects are necessarily funny but because in their pointedness they resemble a joke without actually being one. The person who laughs at them soon gets the point, thereby

Und welche Sprache soll man dann gebrauchen, wenn ein Kunstwerk sich mit äußerster Disziplin jeder überflüssigen Bemerkung enthält? Könnte man einfach ihre Schönheit loben?
Das wäre ein tiefer Sturz in die Falle, die Florian Neufeldt stellt, aber auch darin, in die Falle zu gehen, sind wir frei. Es gibt eine seltsame Schönheit in einem Objekt, dessen einer Bestandteil ein Bündel aus Vierkantstahlrohren ist, die einmal Tischgestelle waren und die sich in ihrem skulpturalen Nachleben seitlich zu Rungen verbinden und so selbst aufrecht halten, deren zweite Komponente jedoch ein LED-Panel ist, das nur deshalb eine funktionale Leuchtquelle sein kann, weil Stahlrohre und Leuchtkörper durch Kabel verbunden sind und erst der Kriechstrom im Metall den Stromkreislauf schließt. Die absichtliche Fehlleitung bringt die Skulptur zum Leuchten. Das Leuchten wiederum ist ihre einzige Funktion. Das Objekt gewinnt durch diese Beschreibung übrigens nichts. Es ist klarer, wenn man von seiner elektrischen Spannung weiß und es bei Wissen und Betrachtung belässt, ohne aus dem einen oder anderen Schlüsse zu ziehen als den, dass Kunst etwas ist, das auf unser Einverständnis vertraut. Es gibt eine Empathie für das Unwahrscheinliche, eine Lust an der Zumutung, eine stillschweigende Konspiration, sich Hohlräume und andere Sinnleerstände zu erobern, ohne sie zu ersticken. Schaut man dem unsichtbaren Kriechstrom zu, ohne etwas zu sagen, könnte man meinen, Neufeldt fordere ebenso stillschweigend, häufiger die Kunst von übereilten Sinnkonstruktionen zu entlasten. Aber das wäre eine billige Spekulation zur Entlastung des Interpreten.
In der zweiten Hälfte dieses Textes werde ich weitere 8500 Zeichen lang einfach schweigen.

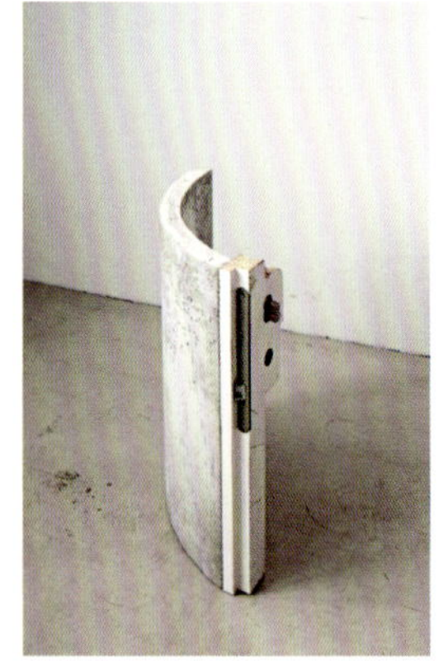
Solidification of Openness (2011)
Holztür, Beton / wooden door, concrete
42 × 42 × 15 cm

recognising the impossibility of analysing and commenting on a punchline. The reflex beats reflection. The observation of the observation process pushes into the space. The ground starts to sway. Does the pleasure of this game exist solely in our freedom to participate? Are we seduced by the fact that there is so little obligation to applaud a roller shutter mounted on the ground for allowing us to temporarily see under the floorboards such that we might unconditionally make a pact with the void, granting us much more space and imposing much more upon us than a cube that is minimalistic in its theatricality? Are Neufeldt's equations appeals to our self-knowledge or rather an exploitation of our over-enthusiasm for the generation of meaning? Are they reflections of our circular thoughts or routes to escape from them, if indeed any thought is possible within them at all, bearing in mind that an equation states no more than what is to be found to the left or right of the equals sign? And what language should we use if a work of art is so wholly disciplined in abstaining from superfluous remarks? Could we simply praise its beauty?

Such would amount to a tremendous tumble headlong into the trap set by Florian Neufeldt, and yet we are at liberty to enter that trap if we please. There is a strange beauty in an object comprised, on the one hand, of a bundle of rectangular steel pipes that, having once belonged to the frame of a table, are joined laterally to posts in their sculptural afterlife and thus kept upright, and, on the other hand, of an LED panel that can only be a functional light source because the steel pipes and light fixtures are joined by cables, and only the leakage current flowing through the metal closes the circuit. The deliberate misrouting causes the sculpture to light up. This is its only function. Incidentally, the object gains nothing from this description. It is more obvious if we are aware of its electrical voltage and if we content ourselves with knowing and observing without trying to draw some kind of conclusion from it beyond the fact that art is something that relies upon our consent. There is an empathy for the improbable, a pleasure in the imposition, a silent conspiracy to conquer cavities and other semantic voids without suffocating them. If we look at the invisible leaking current without saying anything, we could think that Neufeldt is urging us, equally silently, to more frequently safeguard art from overhasty constructions of meaning. But that would be cheap speculation, merely easing the burden on the interpreter. In the second half of this text, I simply remain silent for another 8,500 characters.

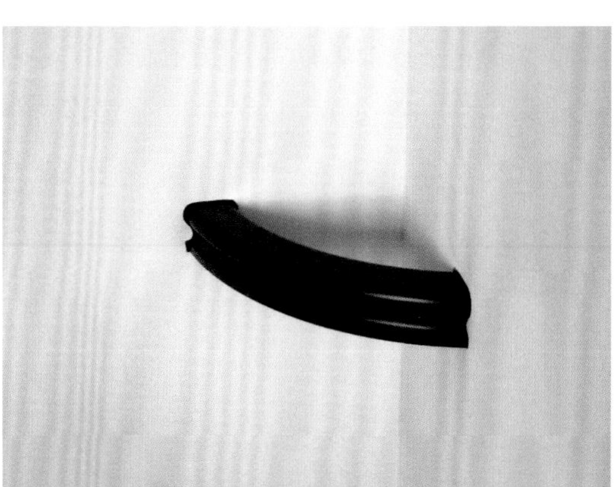

Detail *o. T.* / *Untitled* (2007)
MDF, Lack, Motor, Gipskarton, Holz /
MDF, varnish, motor, drywall, wood
260 × 360 × 360 cm

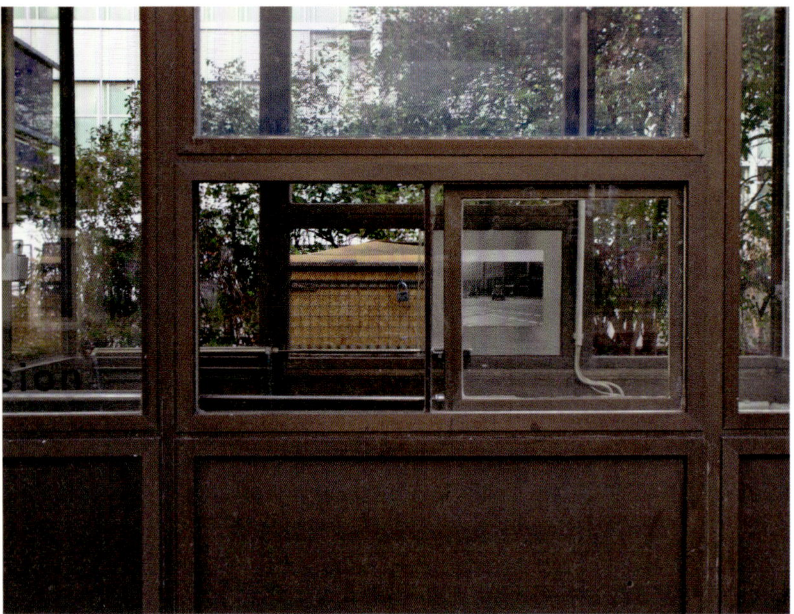

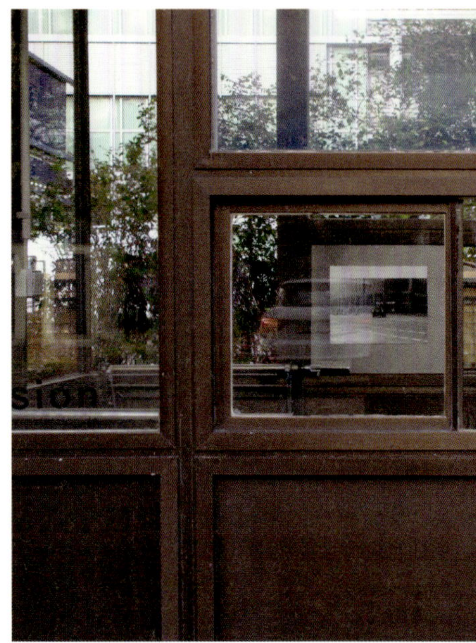

Vehikel (Stoßlüften mit einer Fotografie von Christin Kaiser) /
Vehicle (shock-ventilation with a photo by Christin Kaiser) (2015)
Fotografie, Pneumatikzylinder, Kompressor, Stromgenerator, Schlauch, Kabel /
photo, pneumatic cylinders, compressor, generator, tube, cables

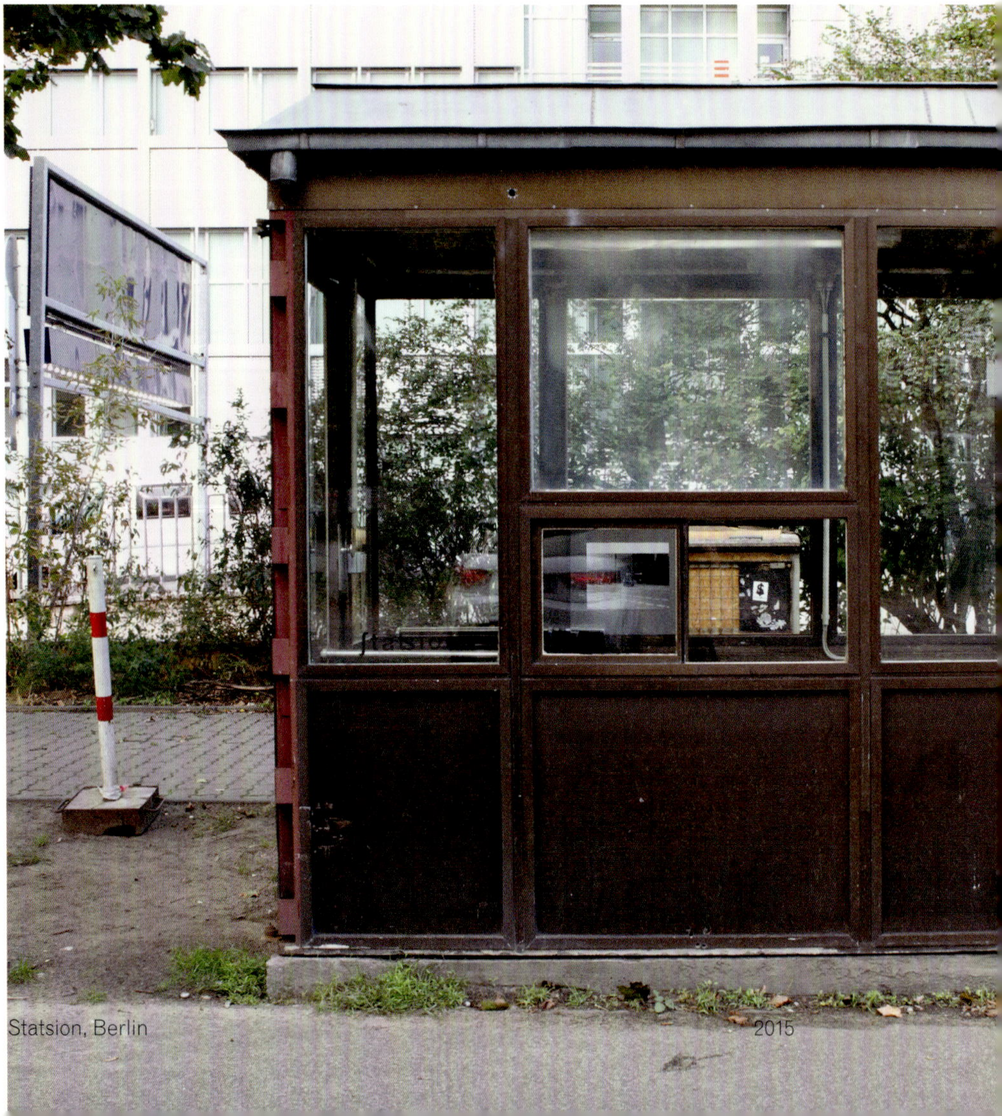

Statsion, Berlin 2015

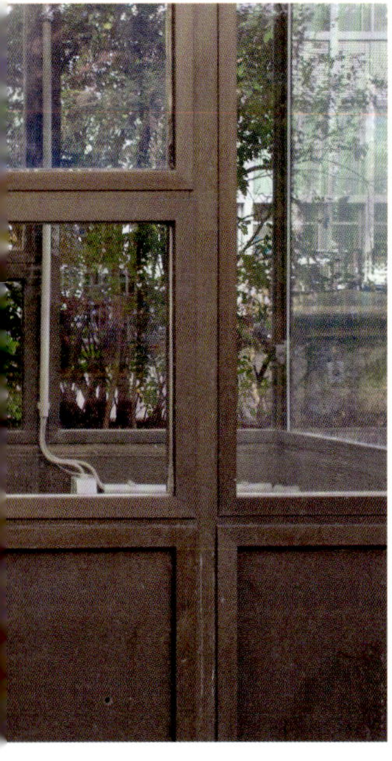

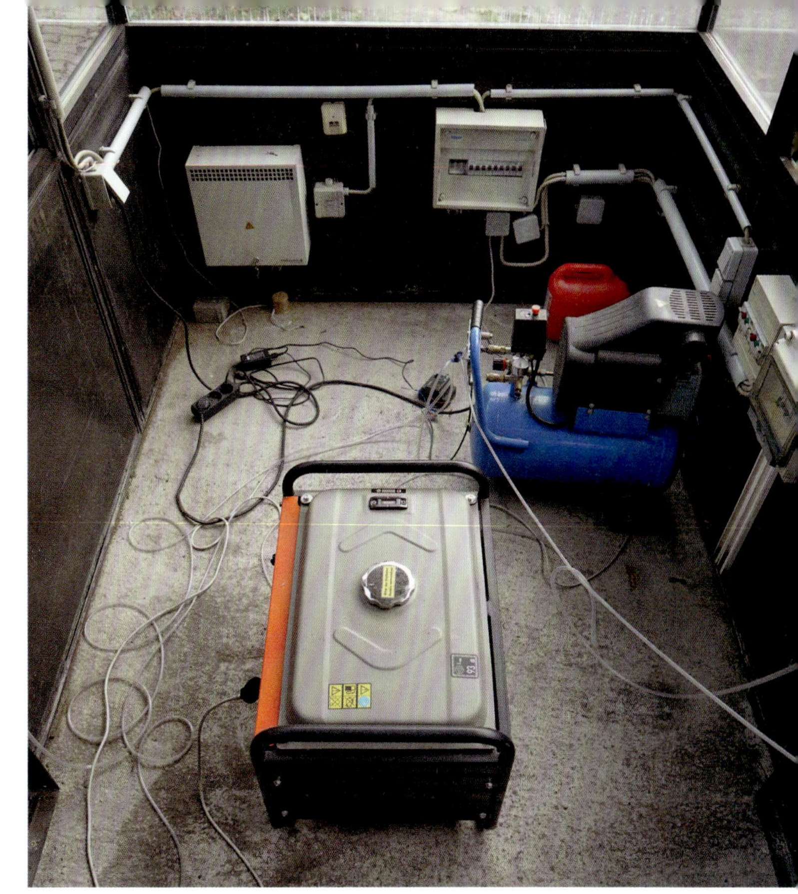

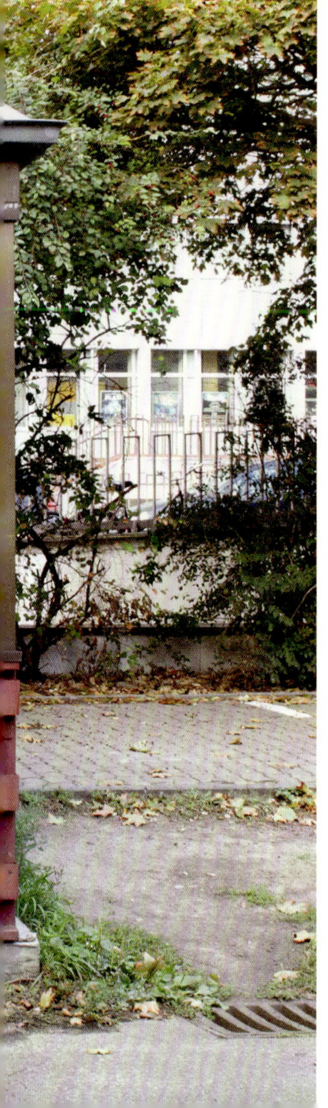

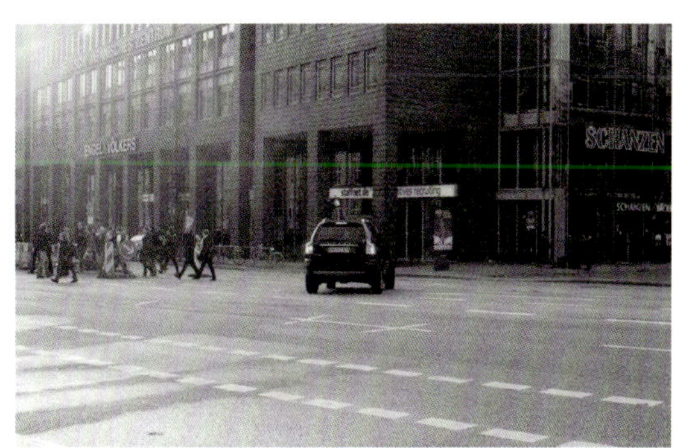
SCHANZEN

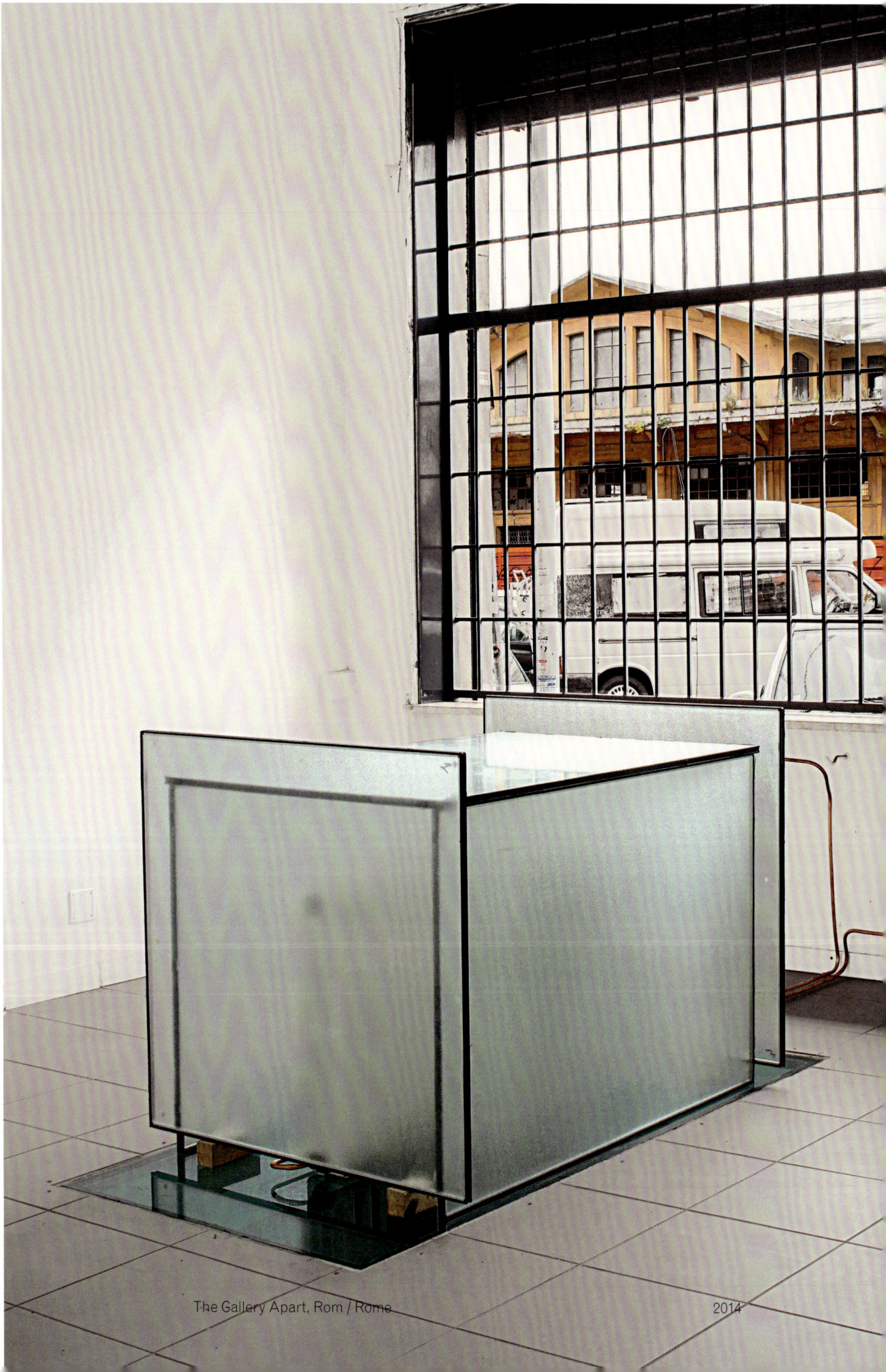

The Gallery Apart, Rom / Rome 2014

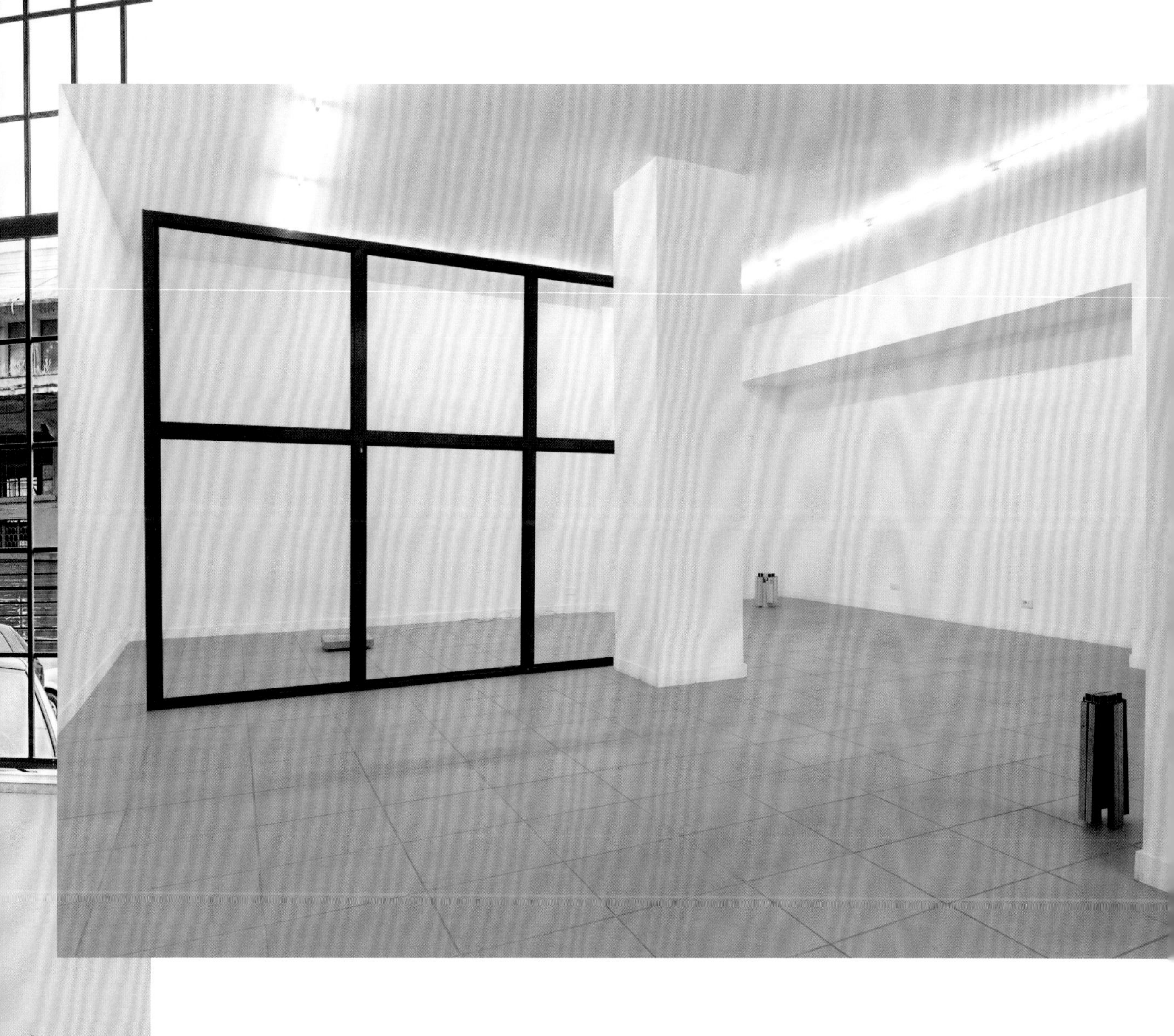

Reassuring a Heater of Its Temperature (2014)
Heizkörper, Fensterglas, Fensterrahmen, Kupferrohr, Holz / heater, window glass, window frame, copper pipe, wood
100 × 160 × 90 cm

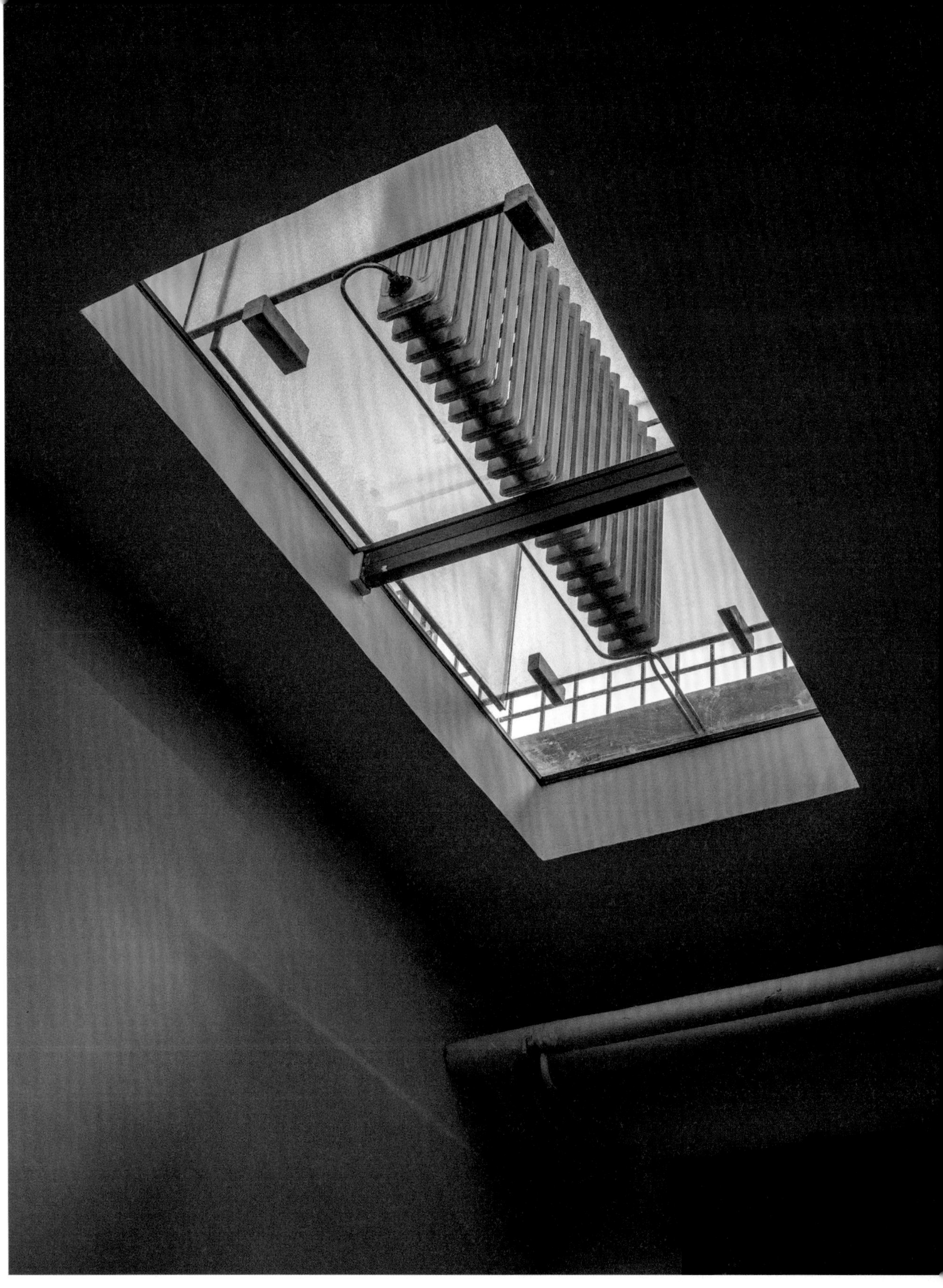

The Gallery Apart, Rom / Rome 2014

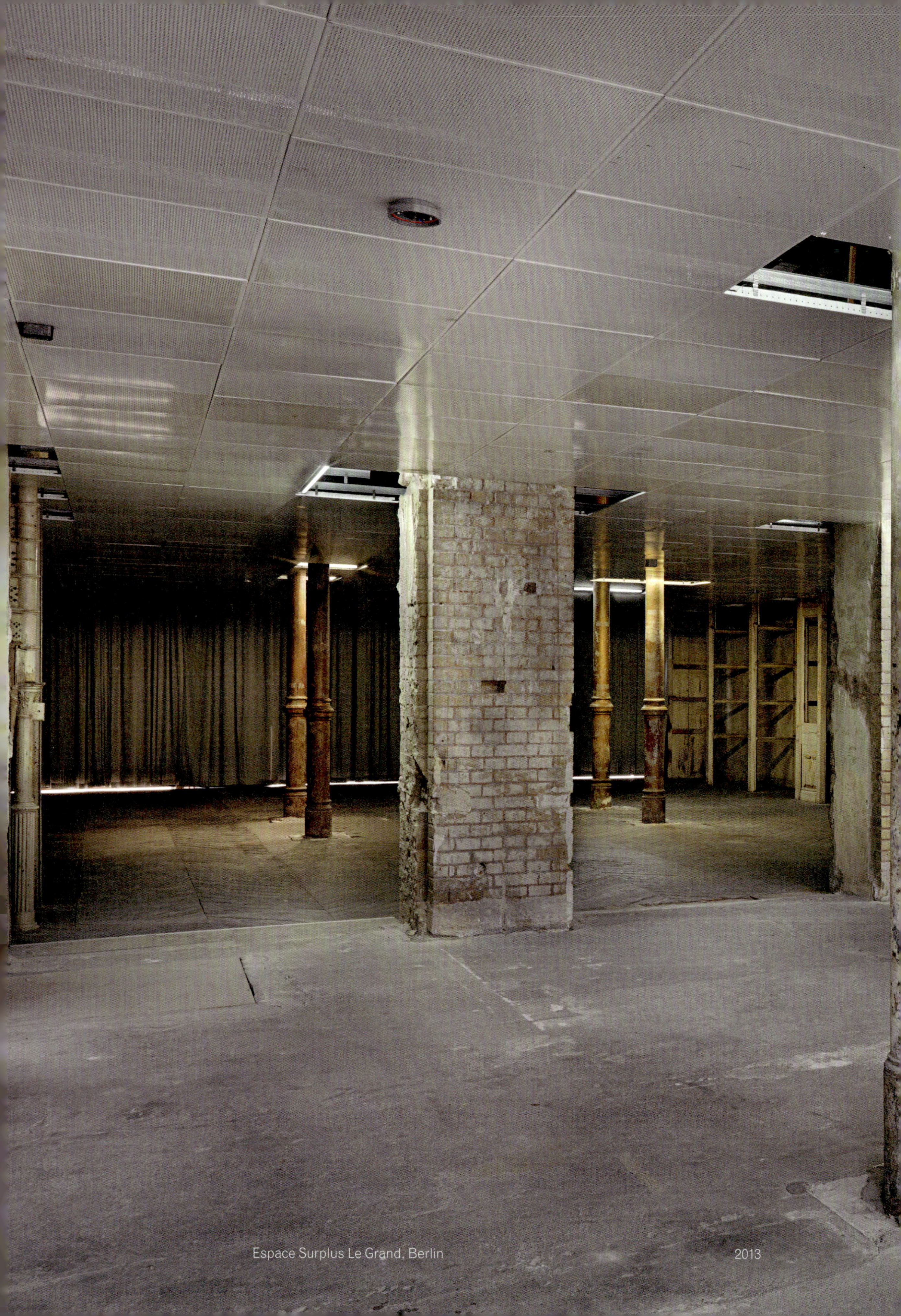

Espace Surplus Le Grand, Berlin 2013

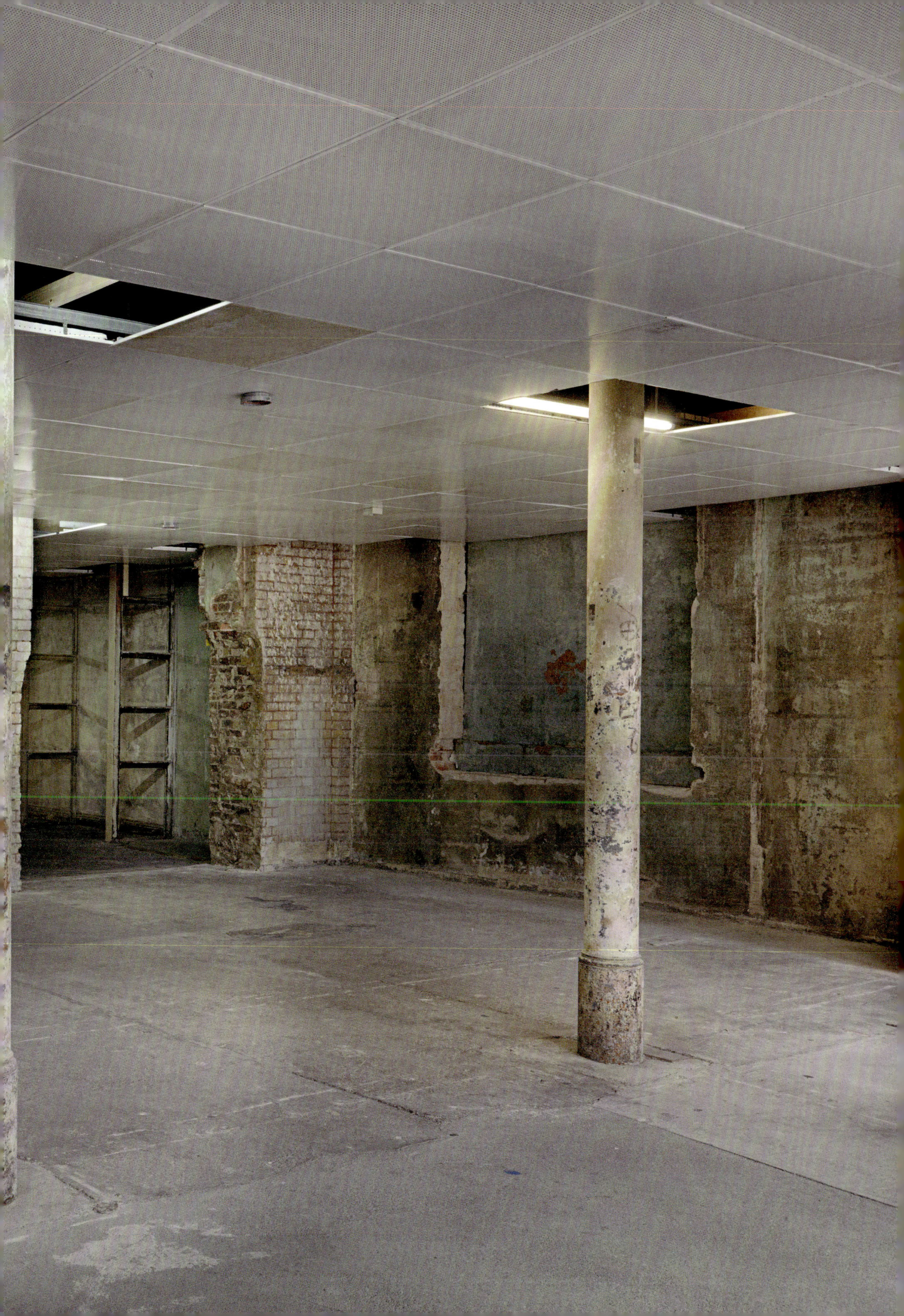

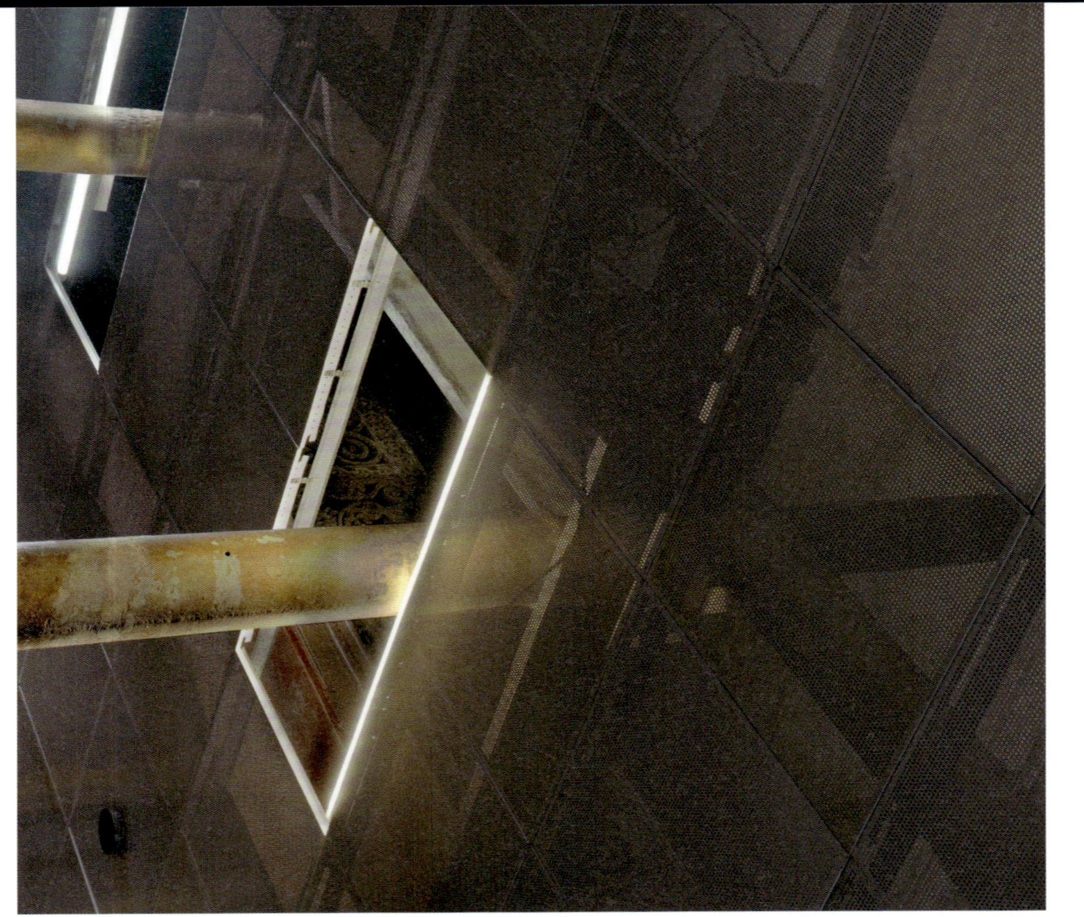

Wechsel der Beleuchtung / Change of Lighting (2013)
Metallblech, Holz, Leuchtstofflampen /
sheet metal, wood, fluorescent lamps
2200 × 1000 cm (Decke / ceiling)

Espace Surplus Le Grand, Berlin 2013

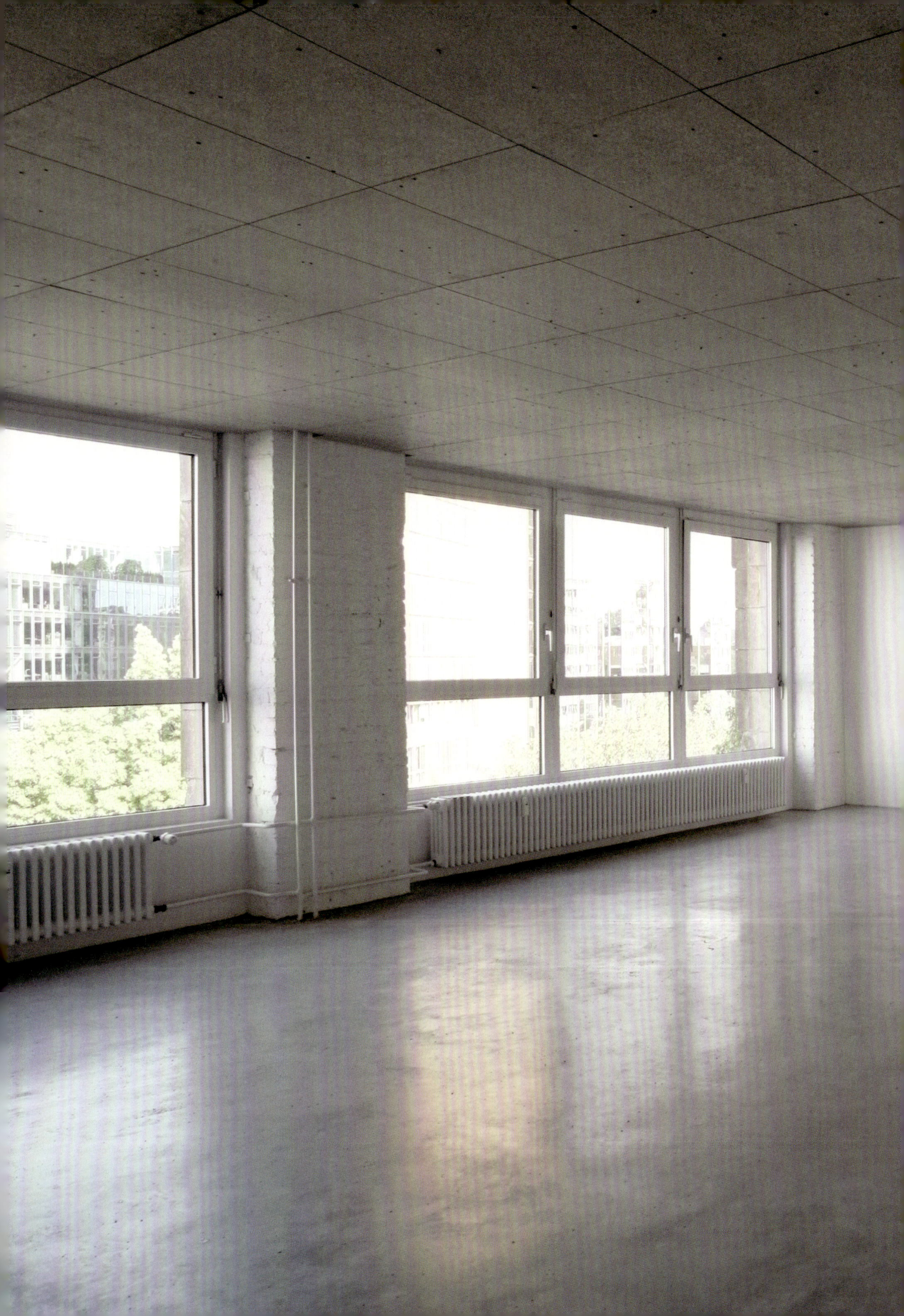

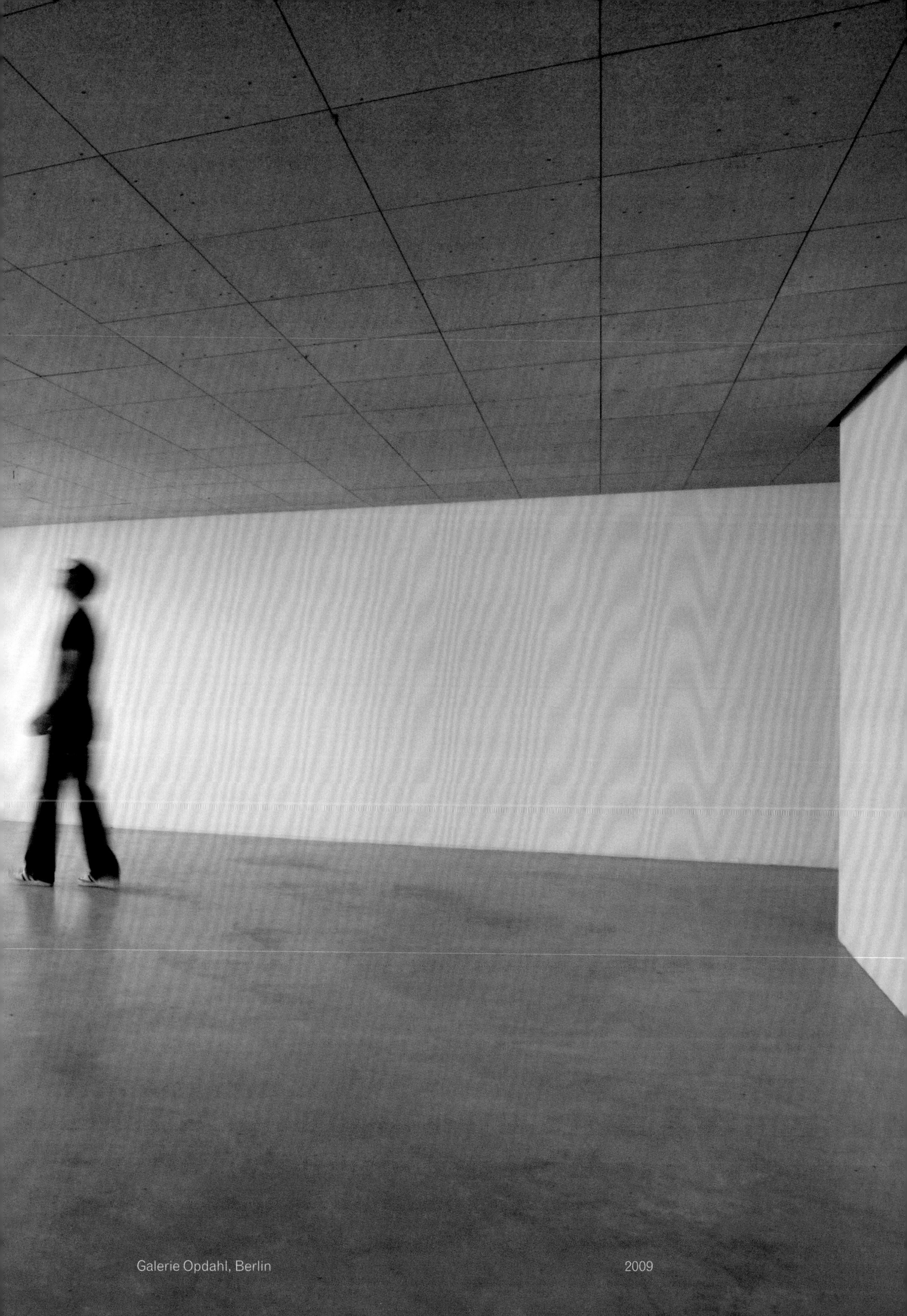

Galerie Opdahl, Berlin 2009

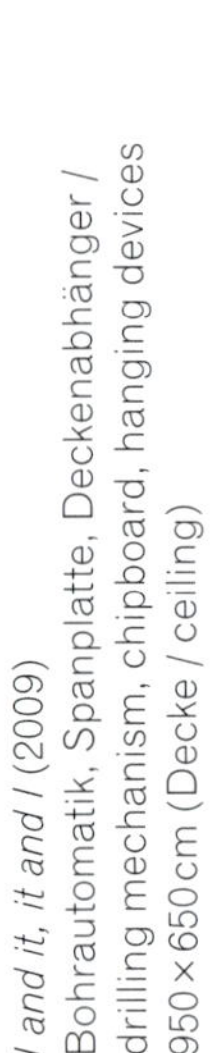

I and it, it and I (2009)
Bohrautomatik, Spanplatte, Deckenabhänger / drilling mechanism, chipboard, hanging devices
950 × 650 cm (Decke / ceiling)

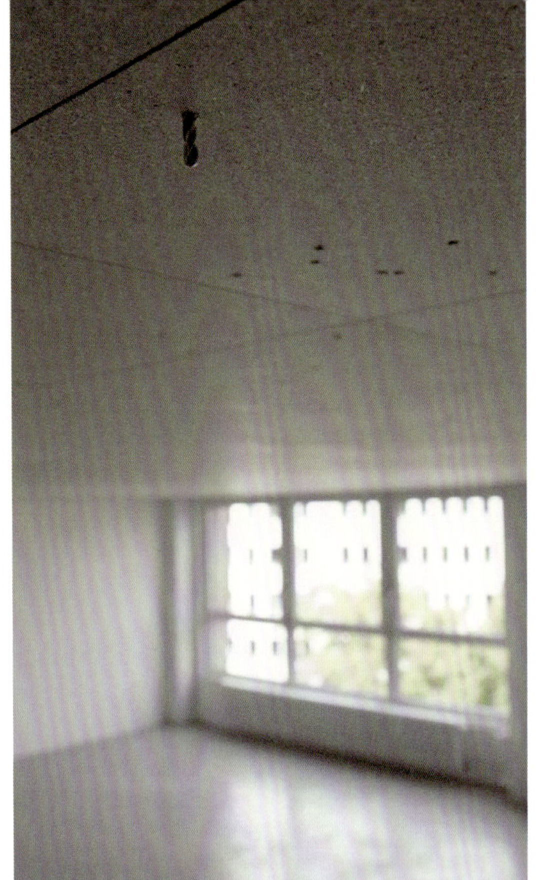

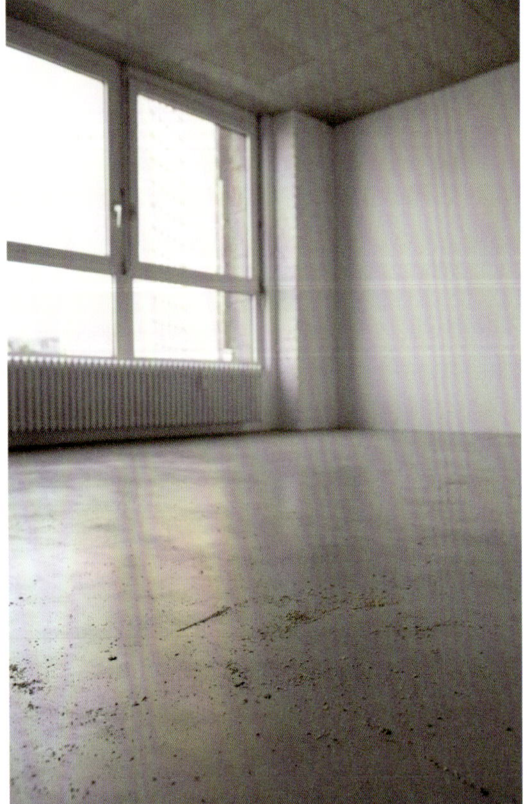

Galerie Opdahl, Berlin

2009

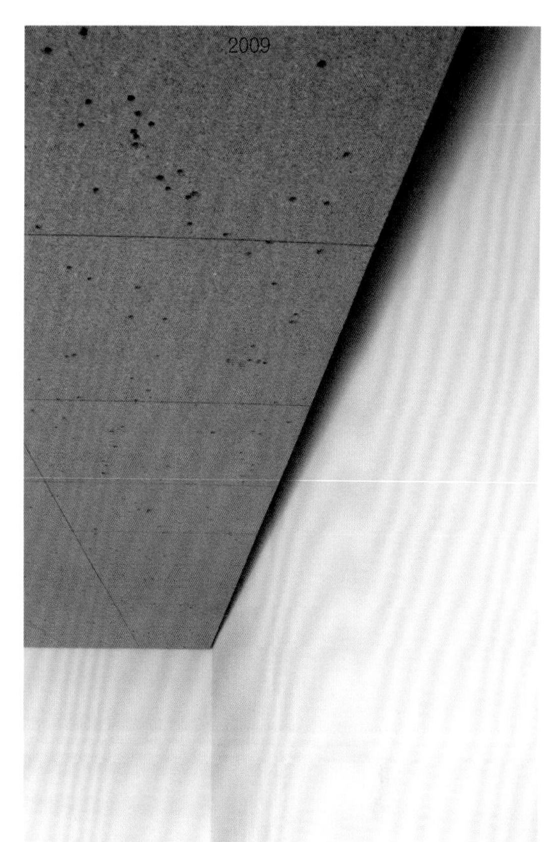

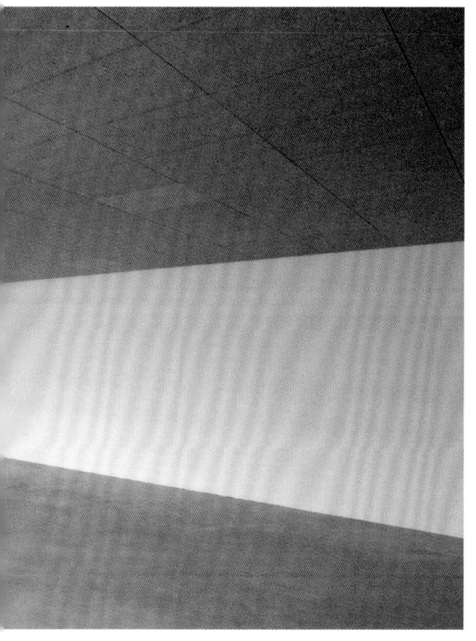

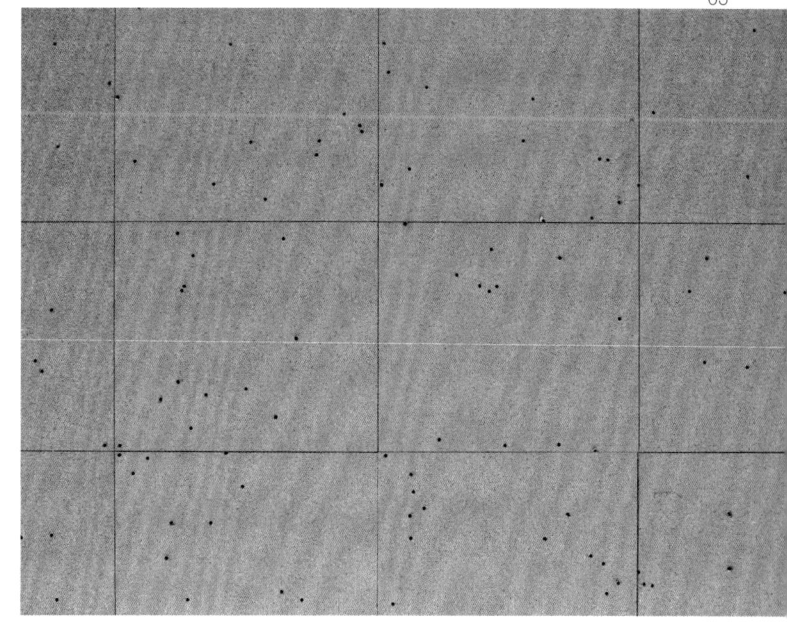

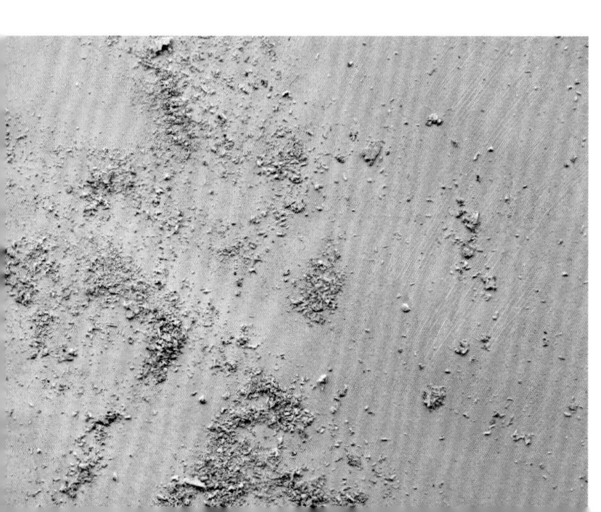

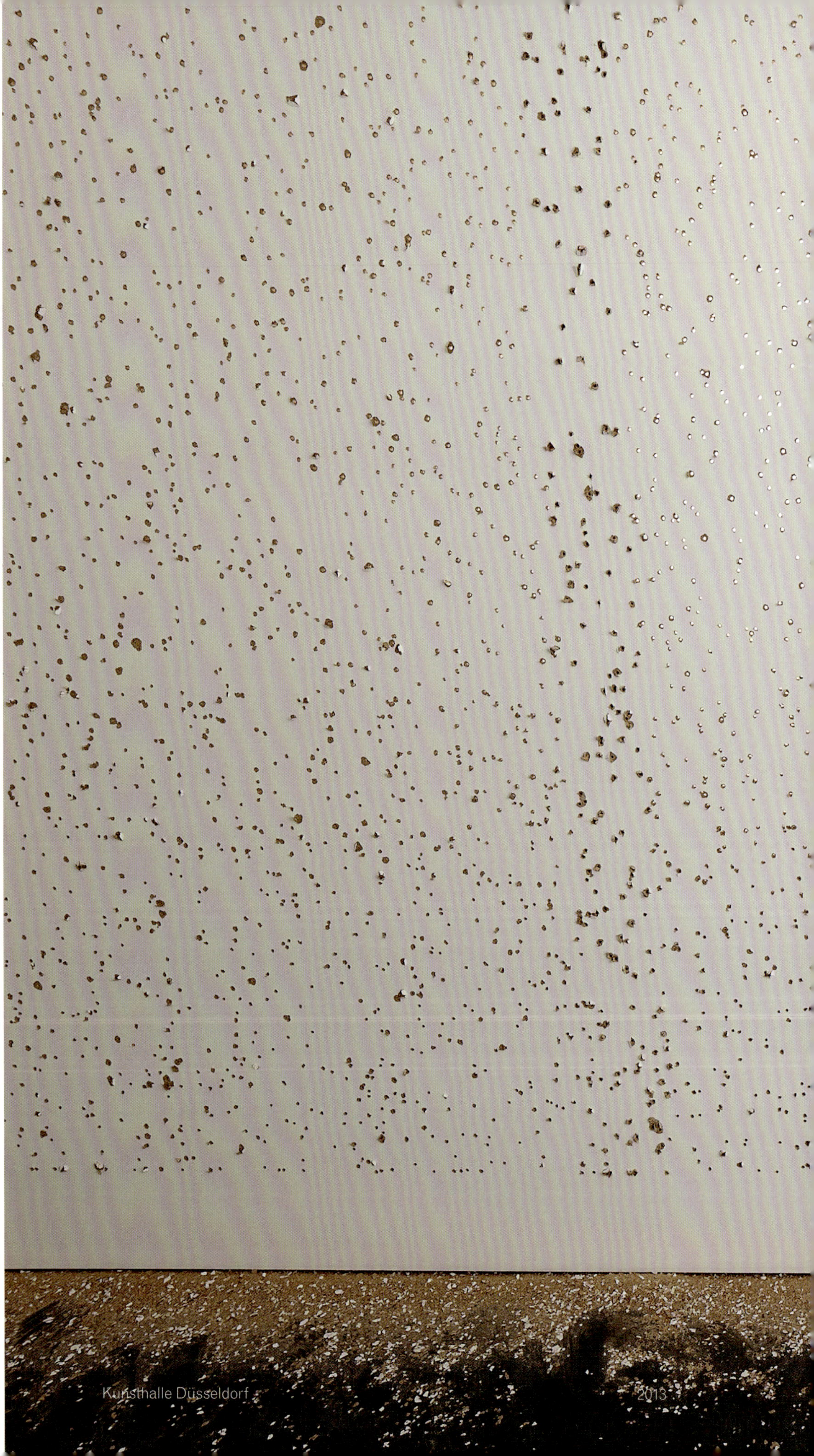

Die Welt durch eine Wand begreifen (2013)
Bohrautomatik, Spanplatte, Holz, Farbe /
drilling mechanism, chipboard, wood, paint
650 × 360 cm

Kunsthalle Düsseldorf 2013

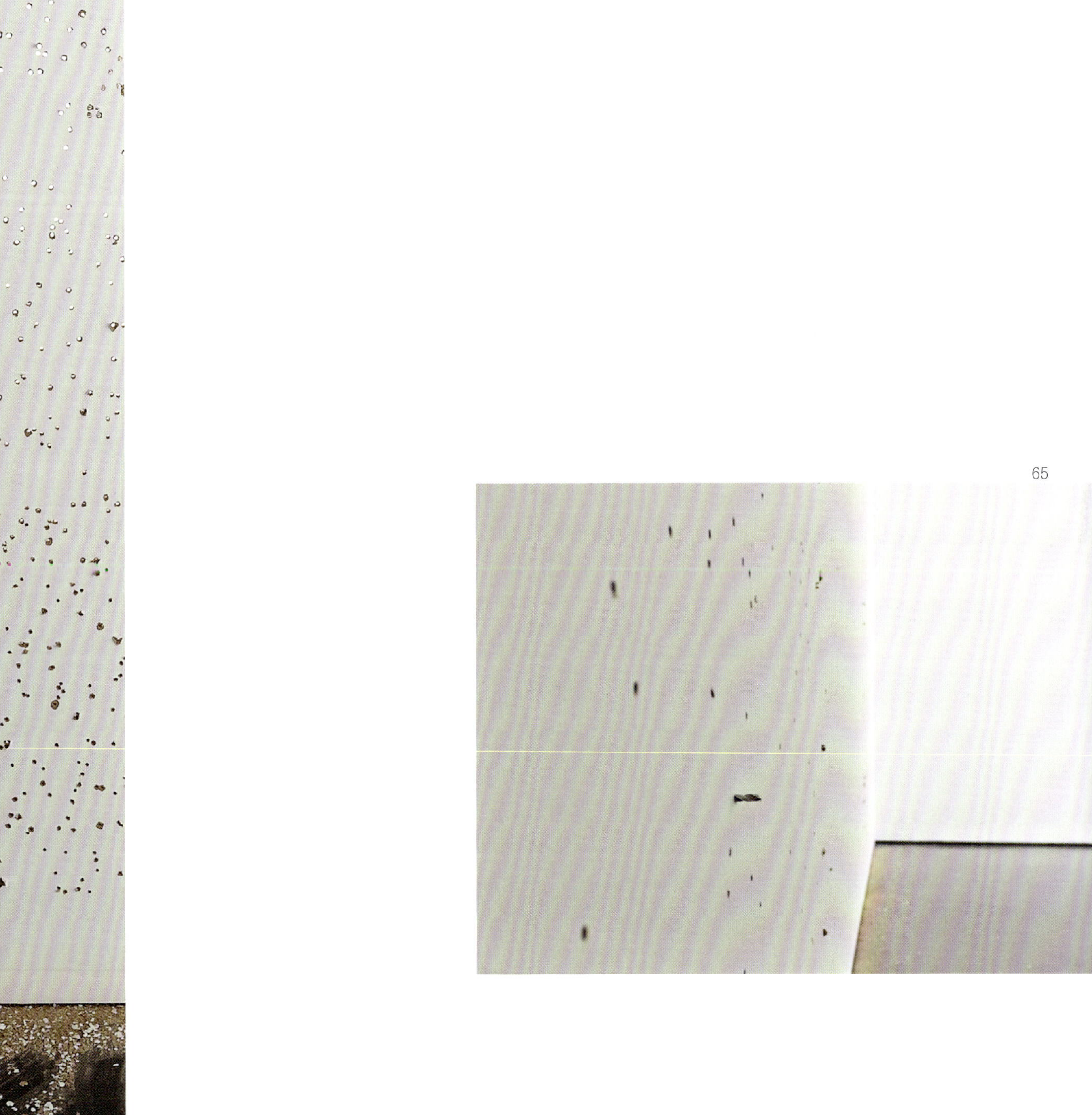

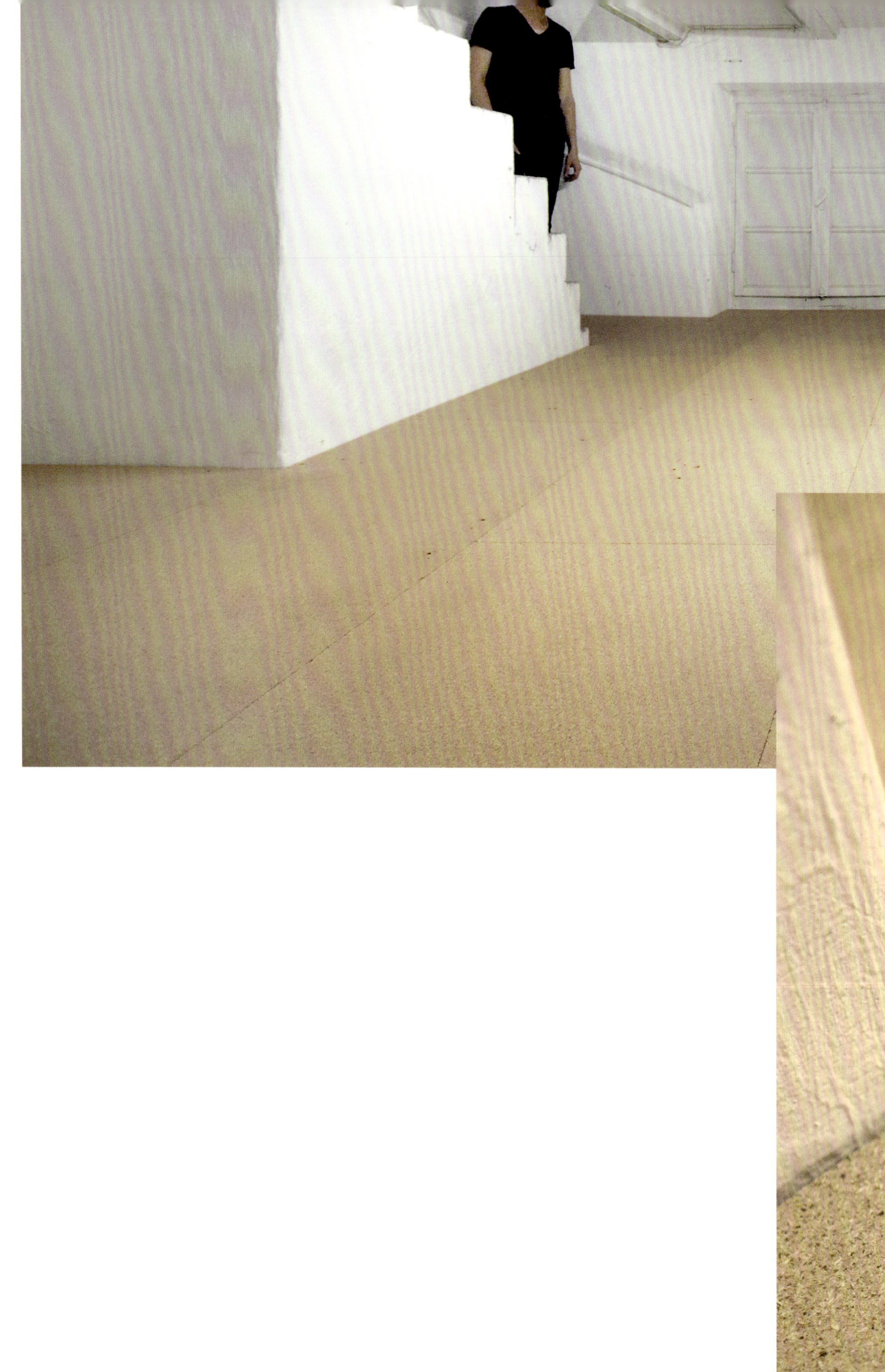

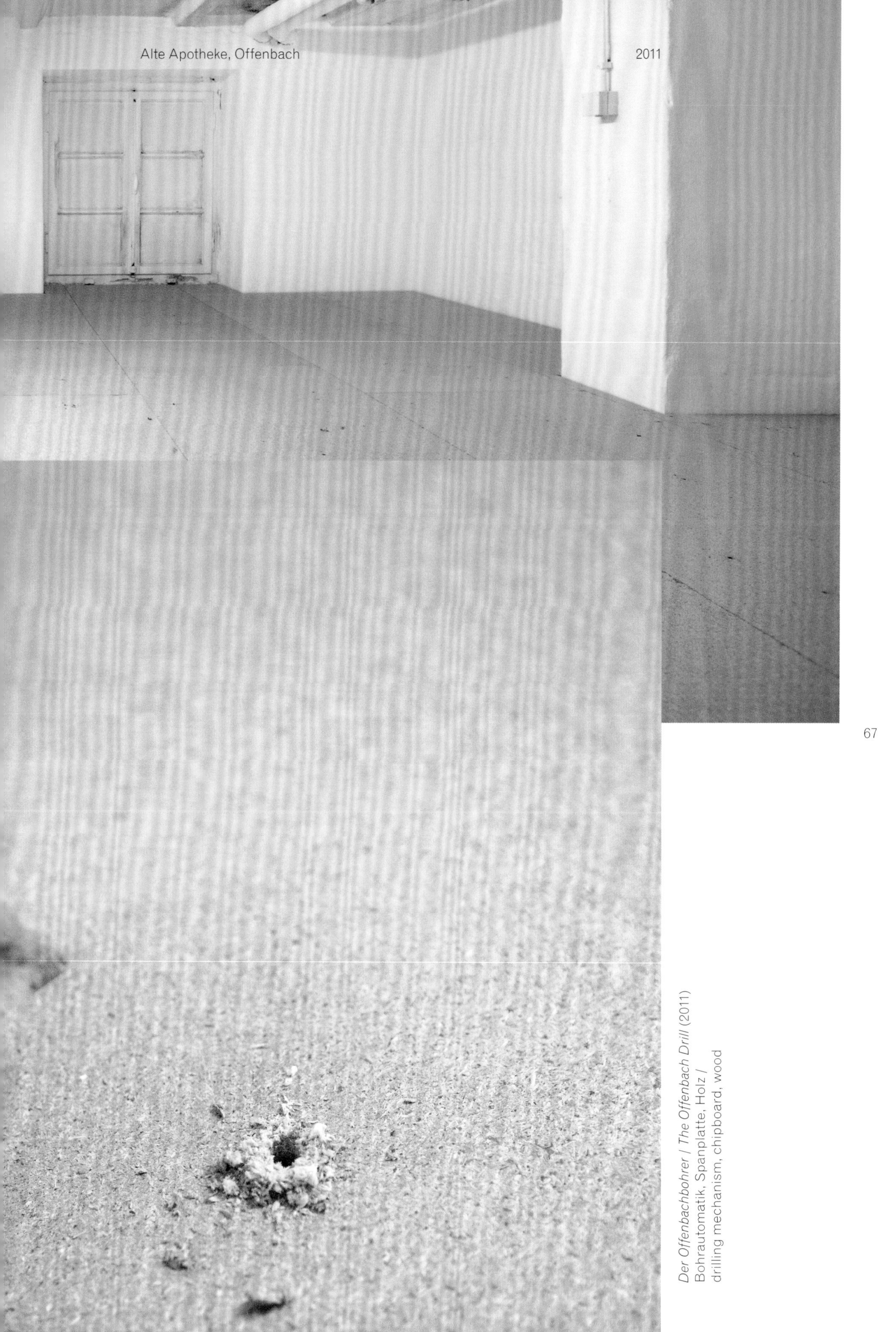

Der Offenbachbohrer / *The Offenbach Drill* (2011)
Bohrautomatik, Spanplatte, Holz /
drilling mechanism, chipboard, wood

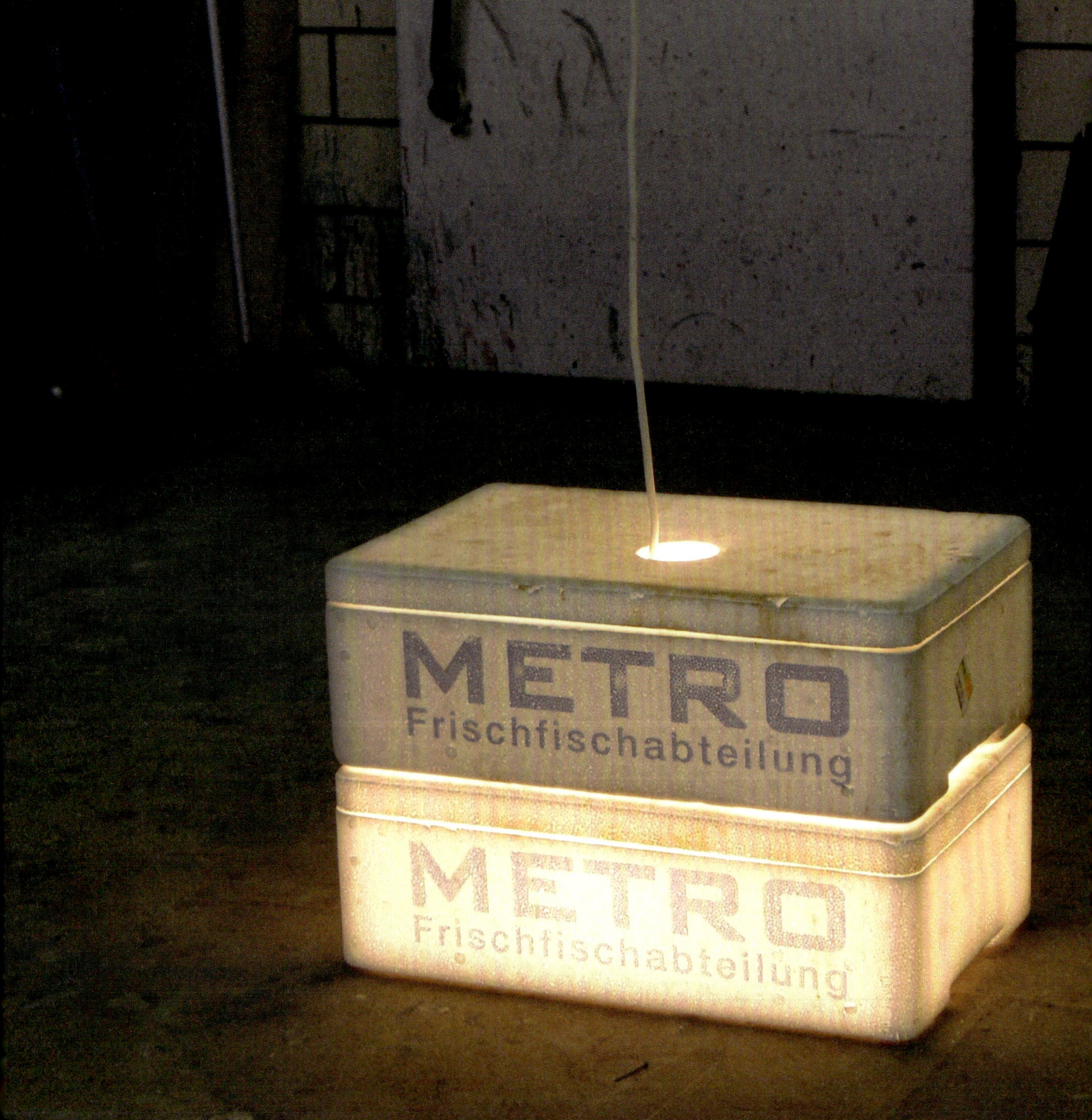
METRO
Frischfischabteilung
METRO
Frischfischabteilung

Atelierskizze / studio sketch
Deep Fishing

Deep Fishing (2018)
Videoprojektion / video projection
16:9 (Loop / loop), 30:22 min

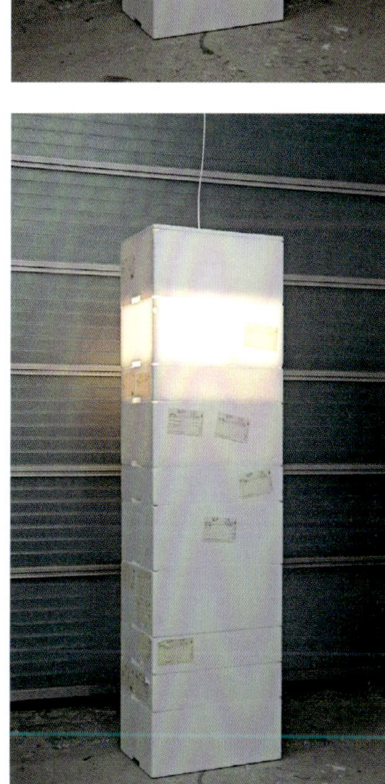

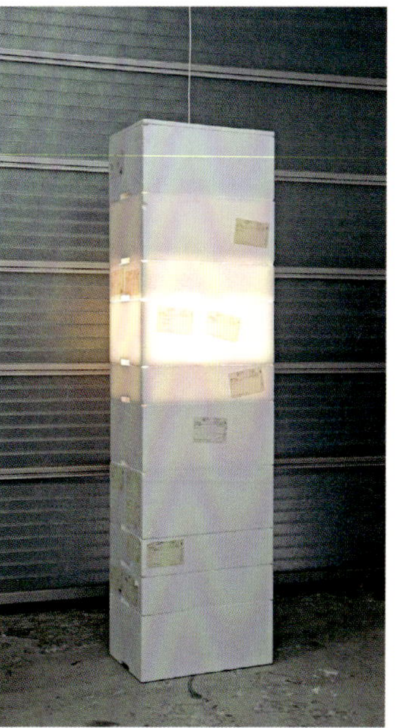

70

Den Boden versuchen / *Trying the Floor* (2012)
Leuchtstoffröhre, Kabel, Vorschaltgerät, Aluminium /
fluorescent tube, cable, control unit, aluminium
4 × 30 × 4 cm (Lampe / lamp)

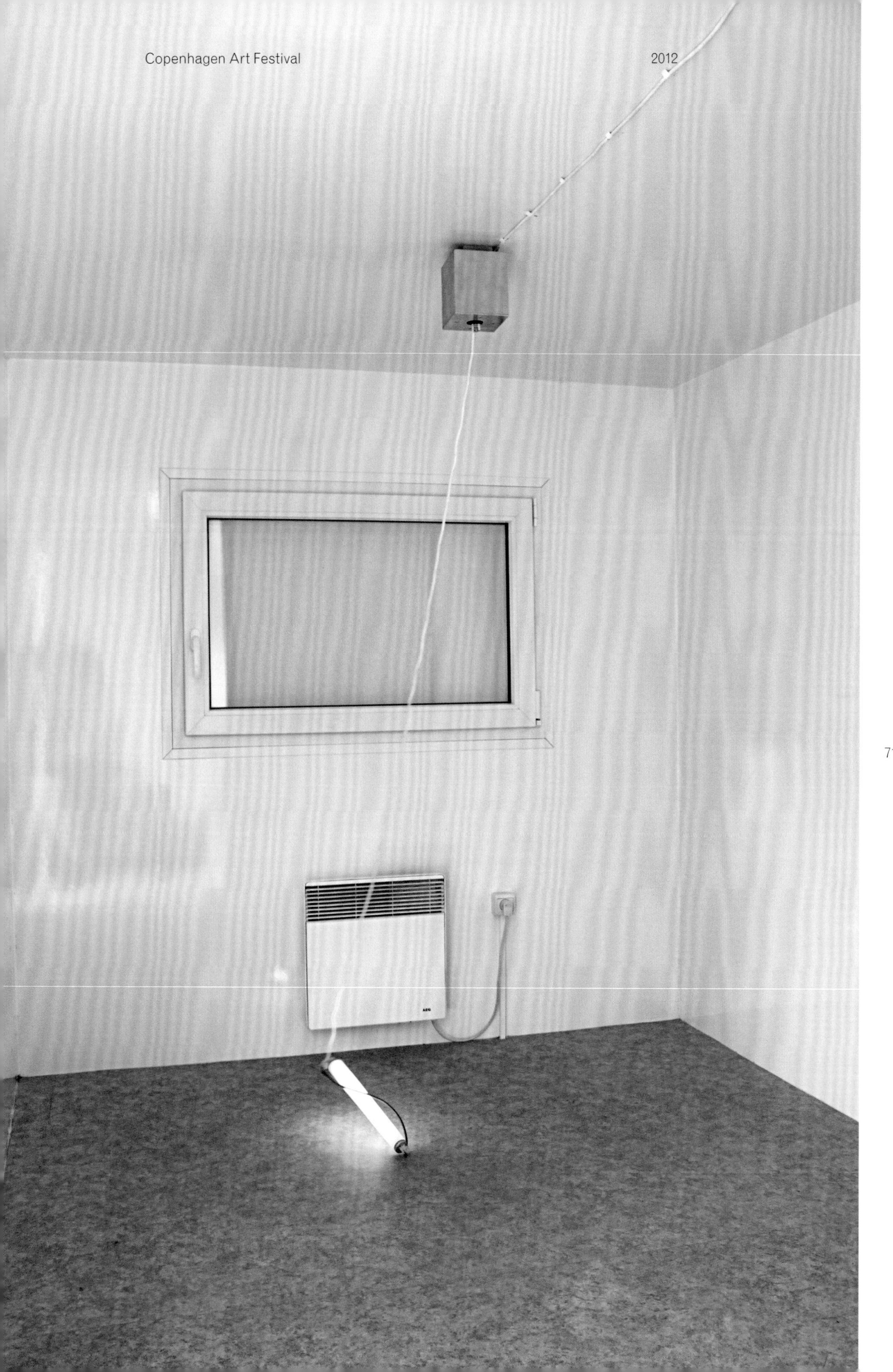

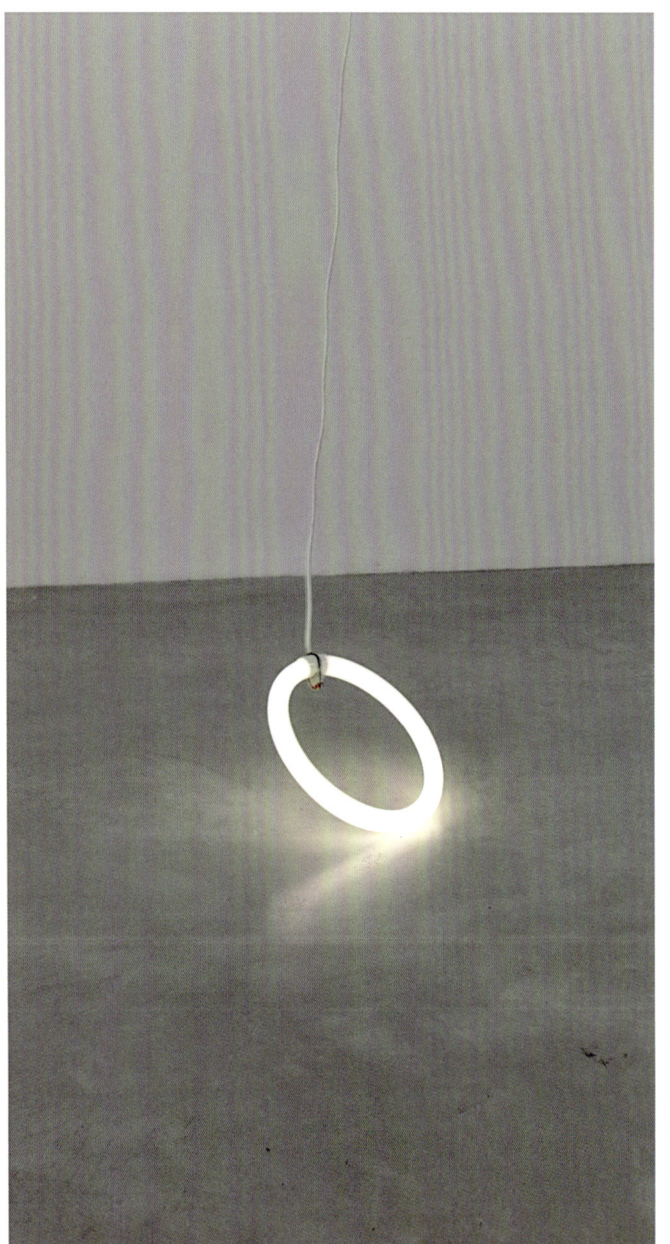

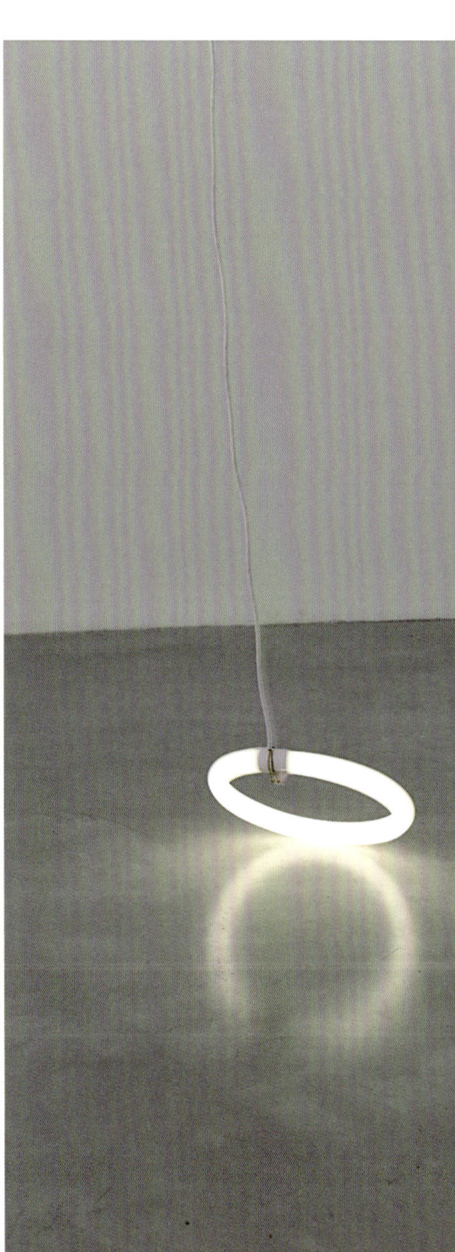

Ungleich Null / Unlike Zero (2008)
Leuchtstoffröhre, Kabel, Vorschaltgerät, Aluminium /
fluorescent tube, cable, control unit, aluminium
ø 30 × 3 cm (Lampe / lamp)

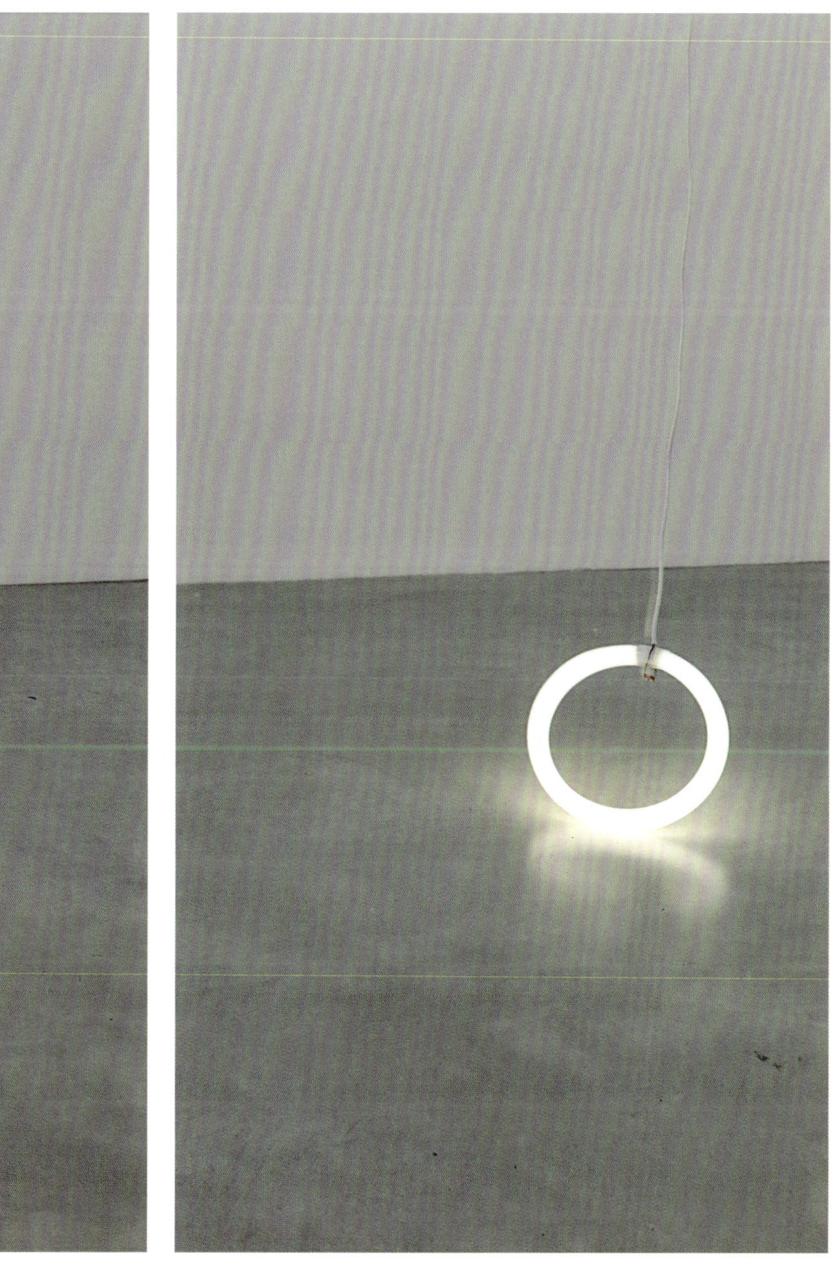

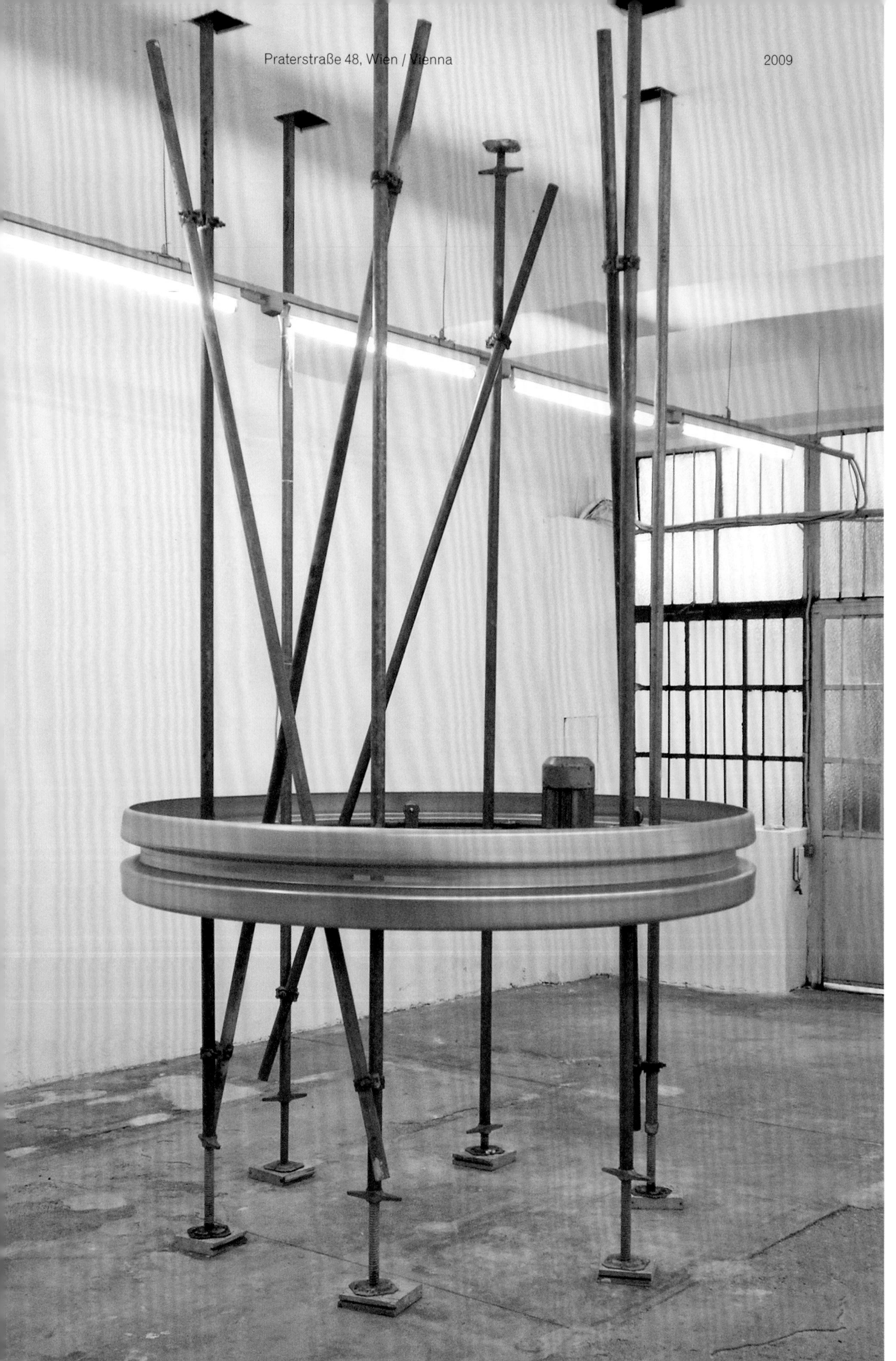

Planke (2007/09)
Leitplanke, Motor, Steuerung, Stahl, Baugerüst /
guardrail, motor, control unit, steel, scaffold
ø 240 × 35 cm (Leitplanke / guardrail)

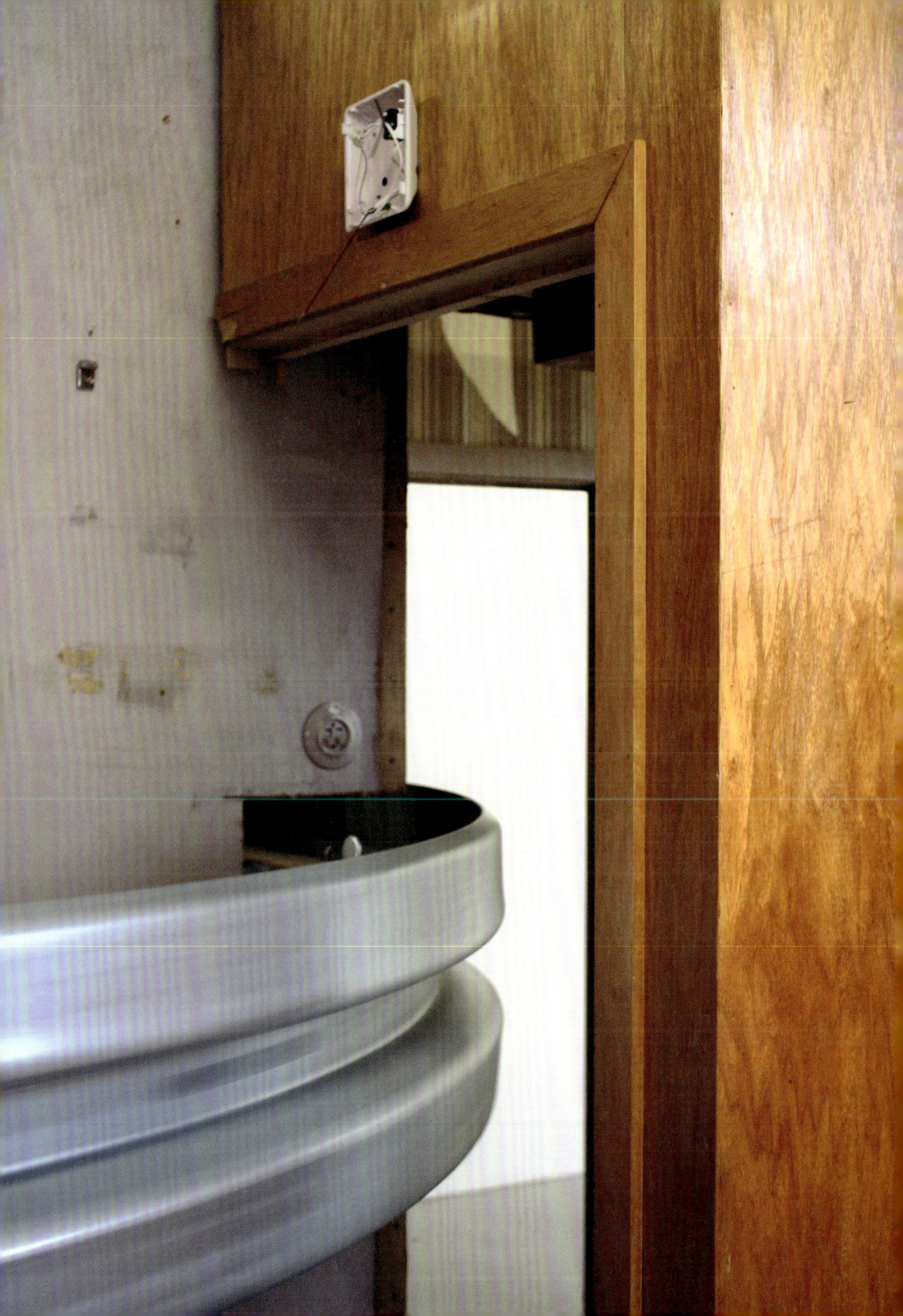

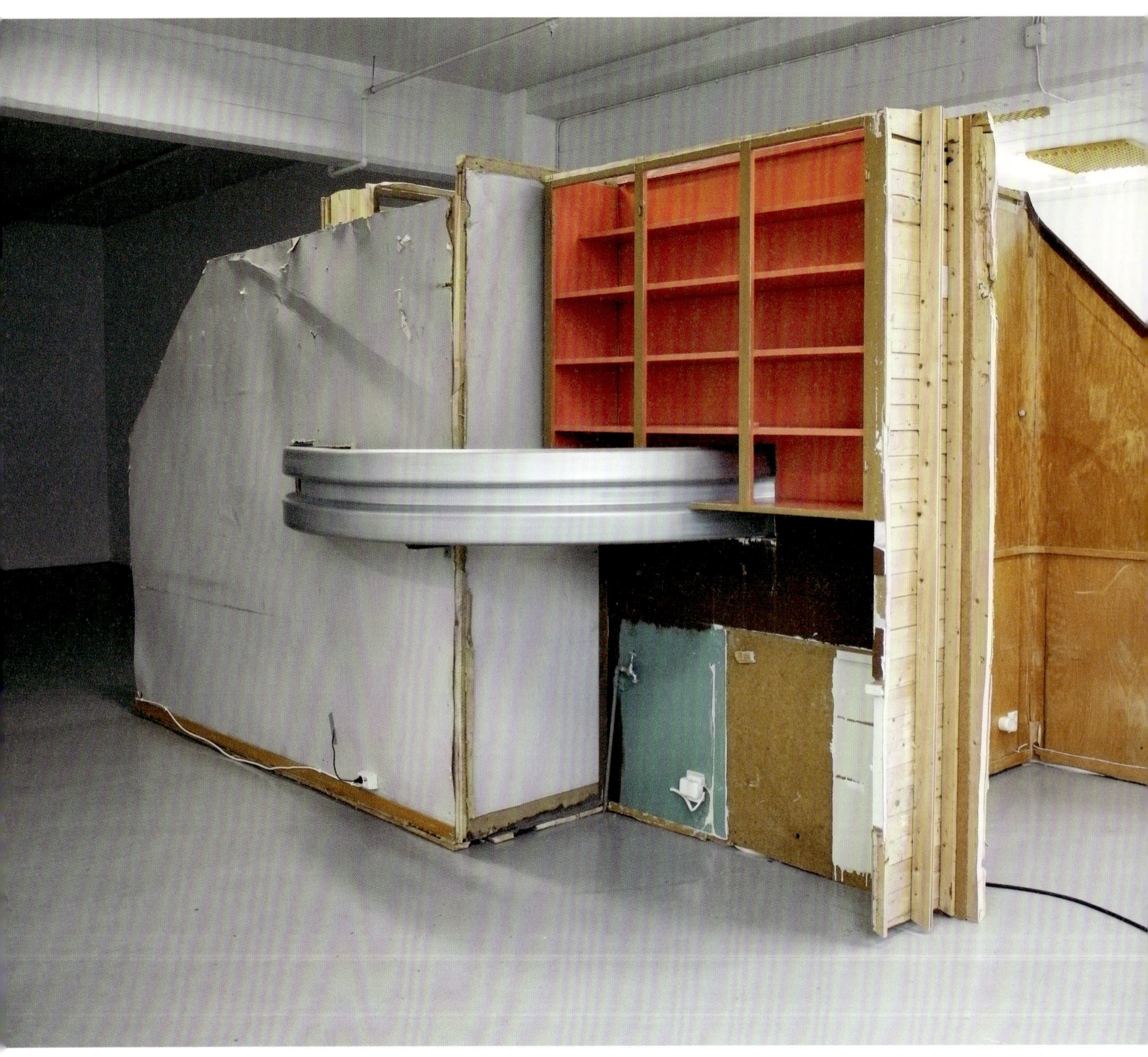

Cuts Both Ways (2010)
Hausteile, Leitplanke, Motor, Steuerung /
house parts, guardrail, motor, wood, control unit
250 × 580 × 630 cm

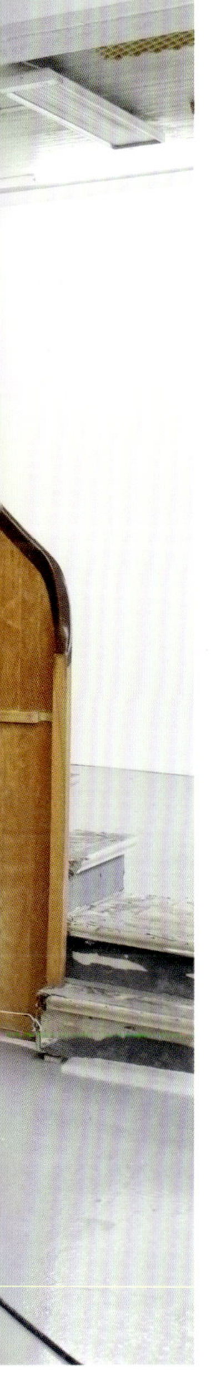

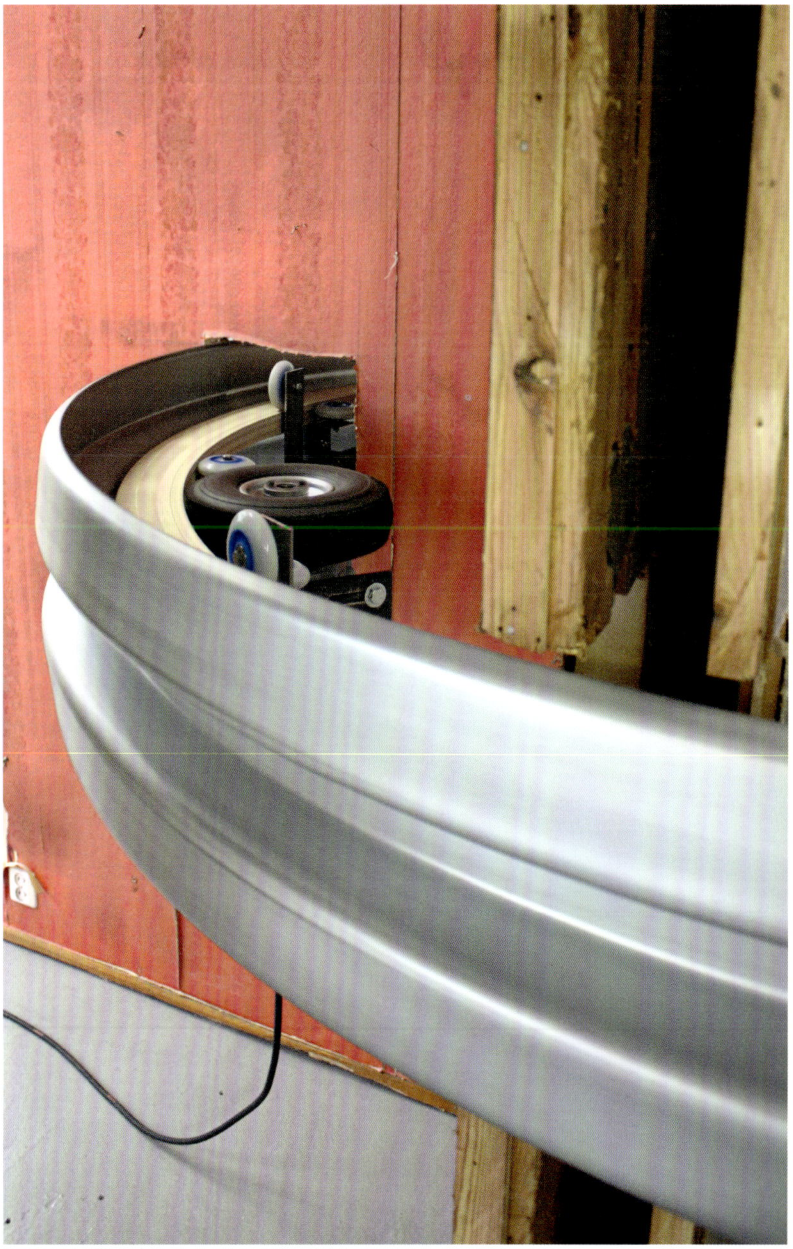

Detail *Cuts Both Ways* (2010)

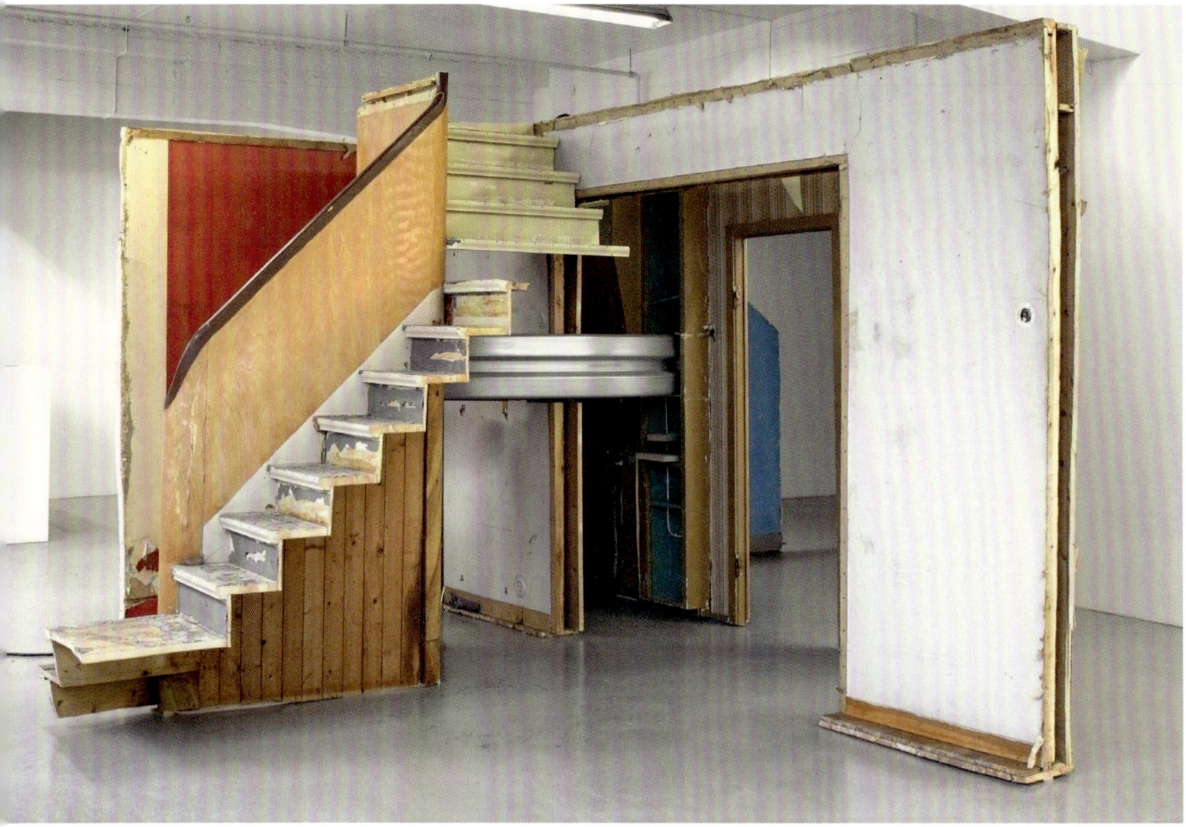

Cuts Both Ways (2010)
Hausteile, Leitplanke, Motor, Steuerung /
house parts, guardrail, motor, control unit
250 × 580 × 630 cm

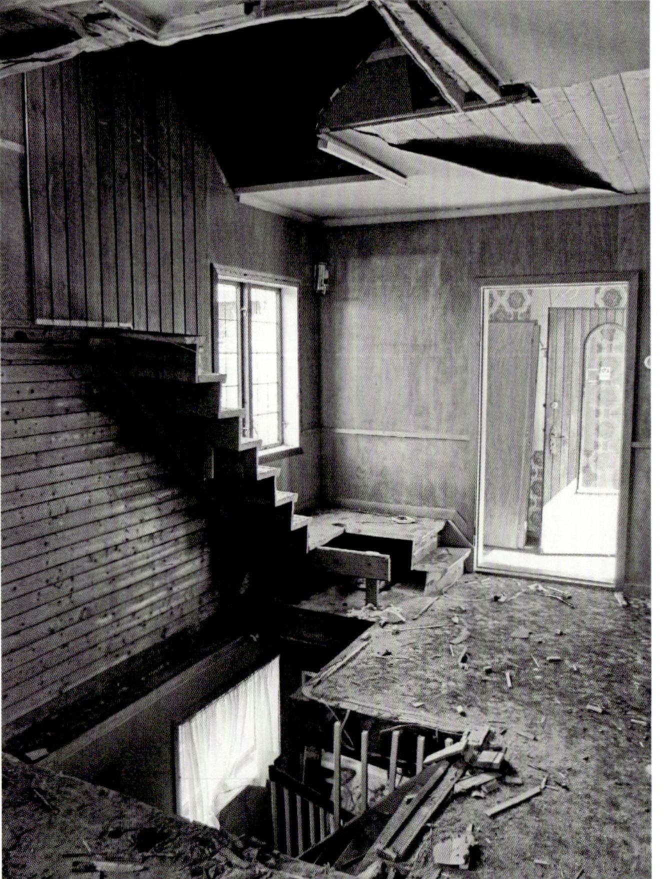

Blick in das Haus in Stavanger, dem die Wände entnommen wurden /
view into the house in Stavanger out of which the parts were taken

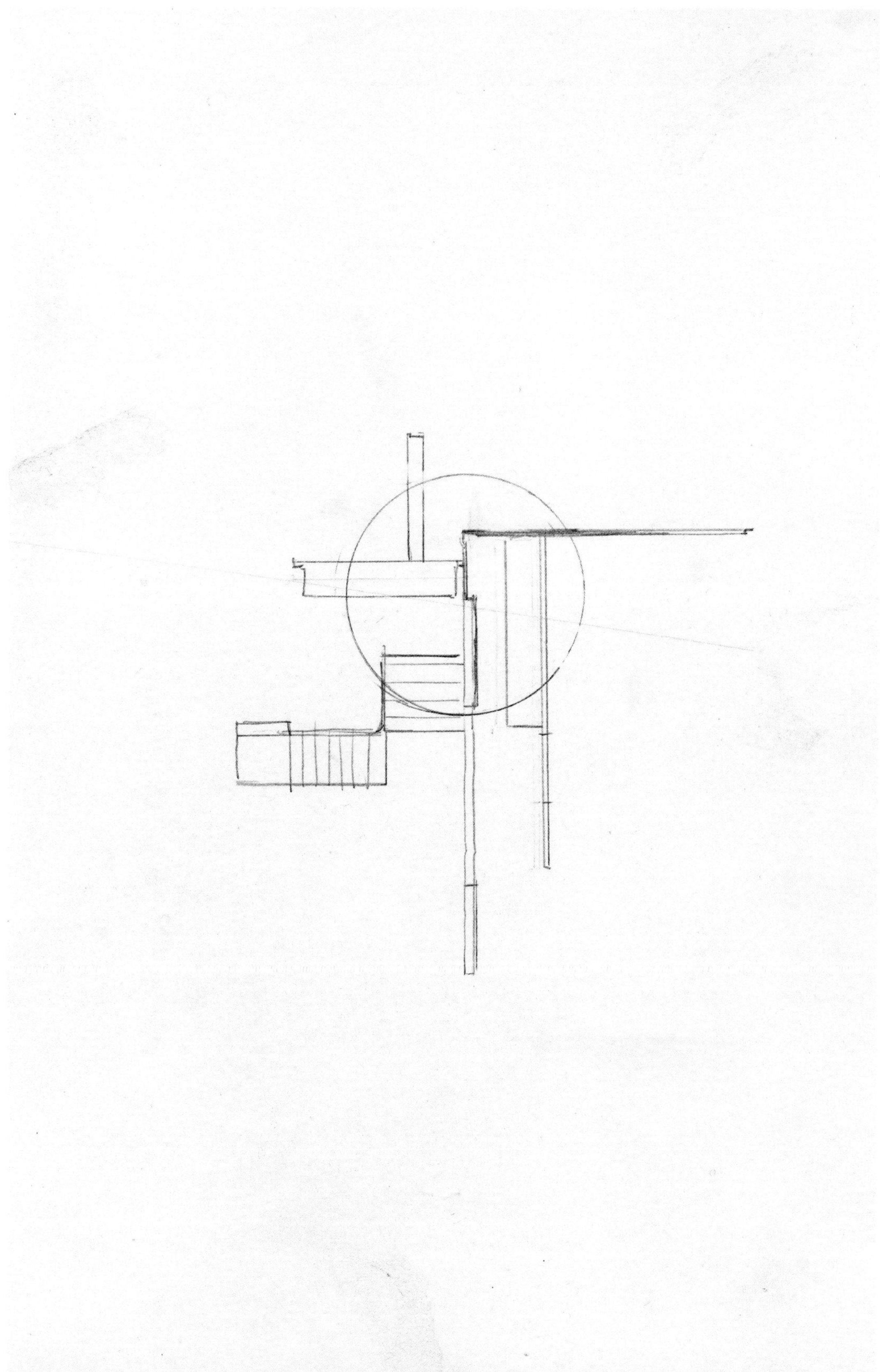

Skizze / sketch *Cuts Both Ways* (2010)
29,6 × 21 cm

Quelques coins et un cercle (2011)
Leitplanke, Motor, Steuerung, Stahl, Holz /
guardrail, motor, control unit, steel, wood
⌀ 240 × 35 cm (Leitplanke / guardrail)

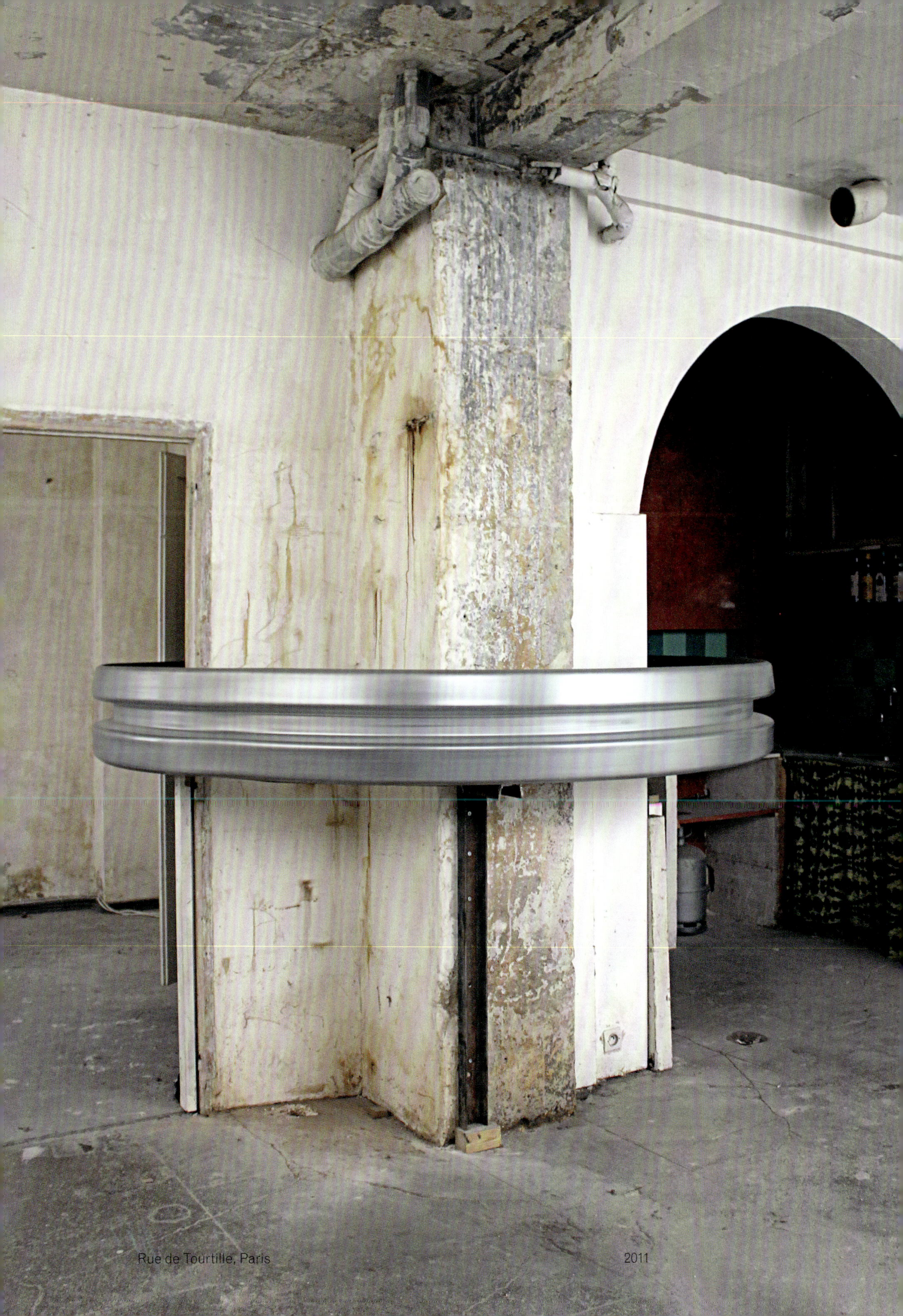

Rue de Tourtille, Paris 2011

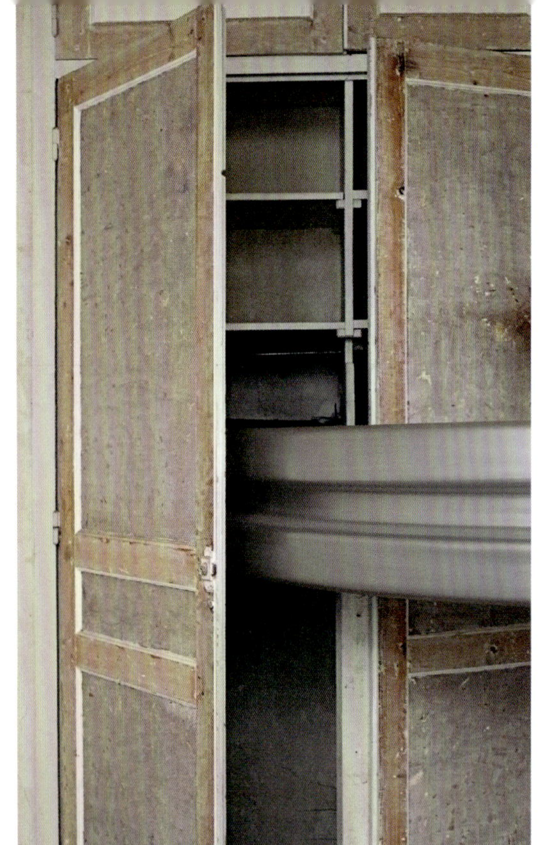

Quelques coins et un cercle (2011)
Leitplanke, Motor, Steuerung, Stahl, Holz / guardrail, motor, control unit, steel, wood
ø 240 × 35 cm (Leitplanke / guardrail)

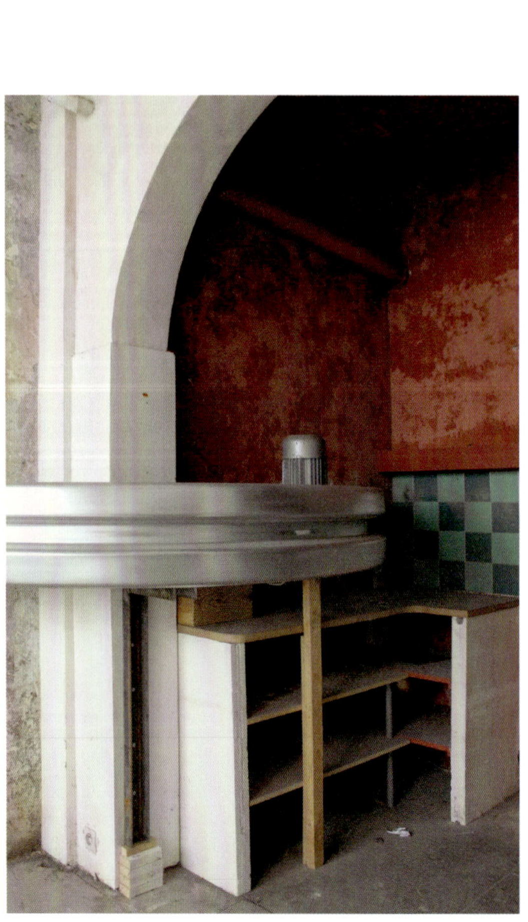

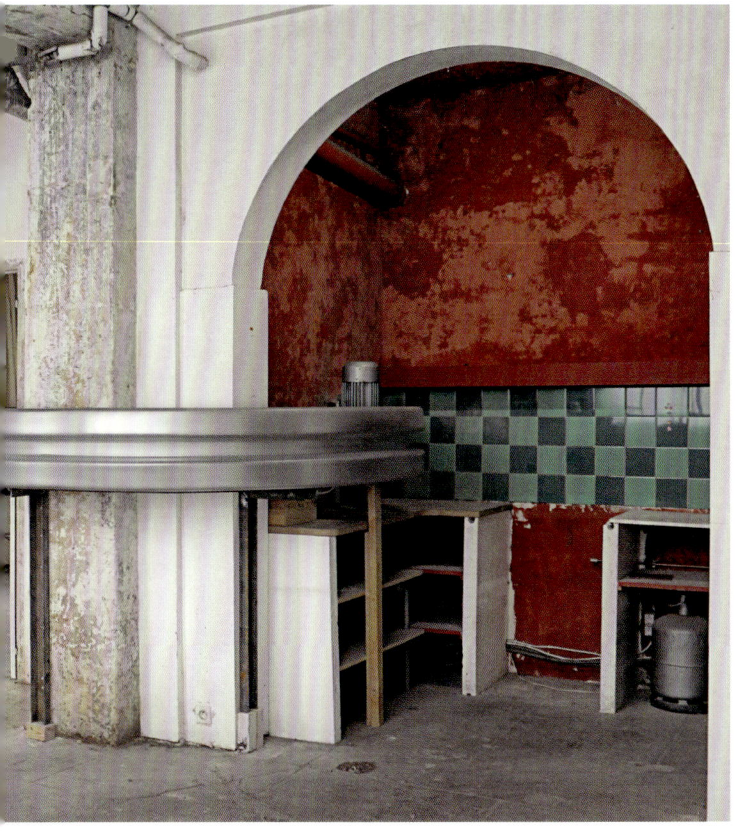

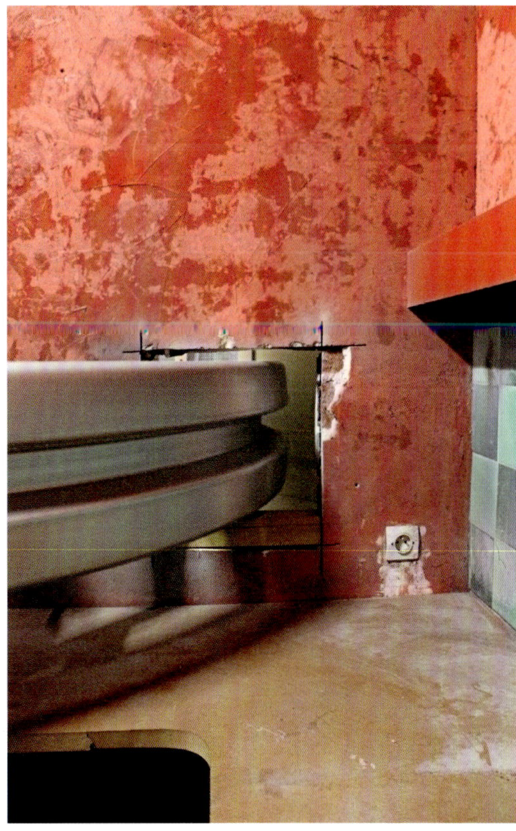

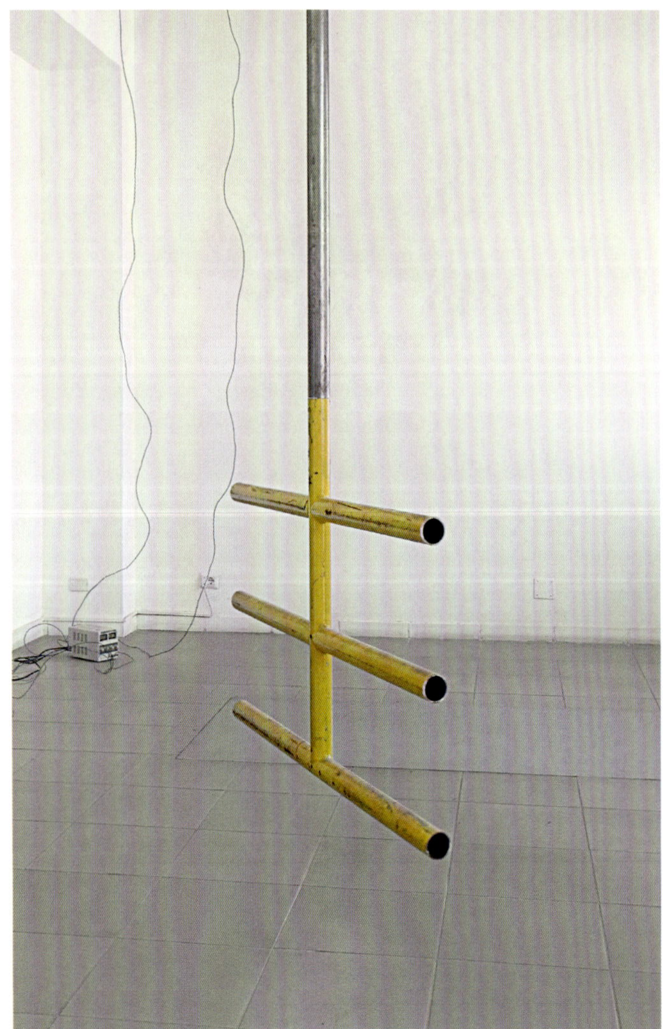

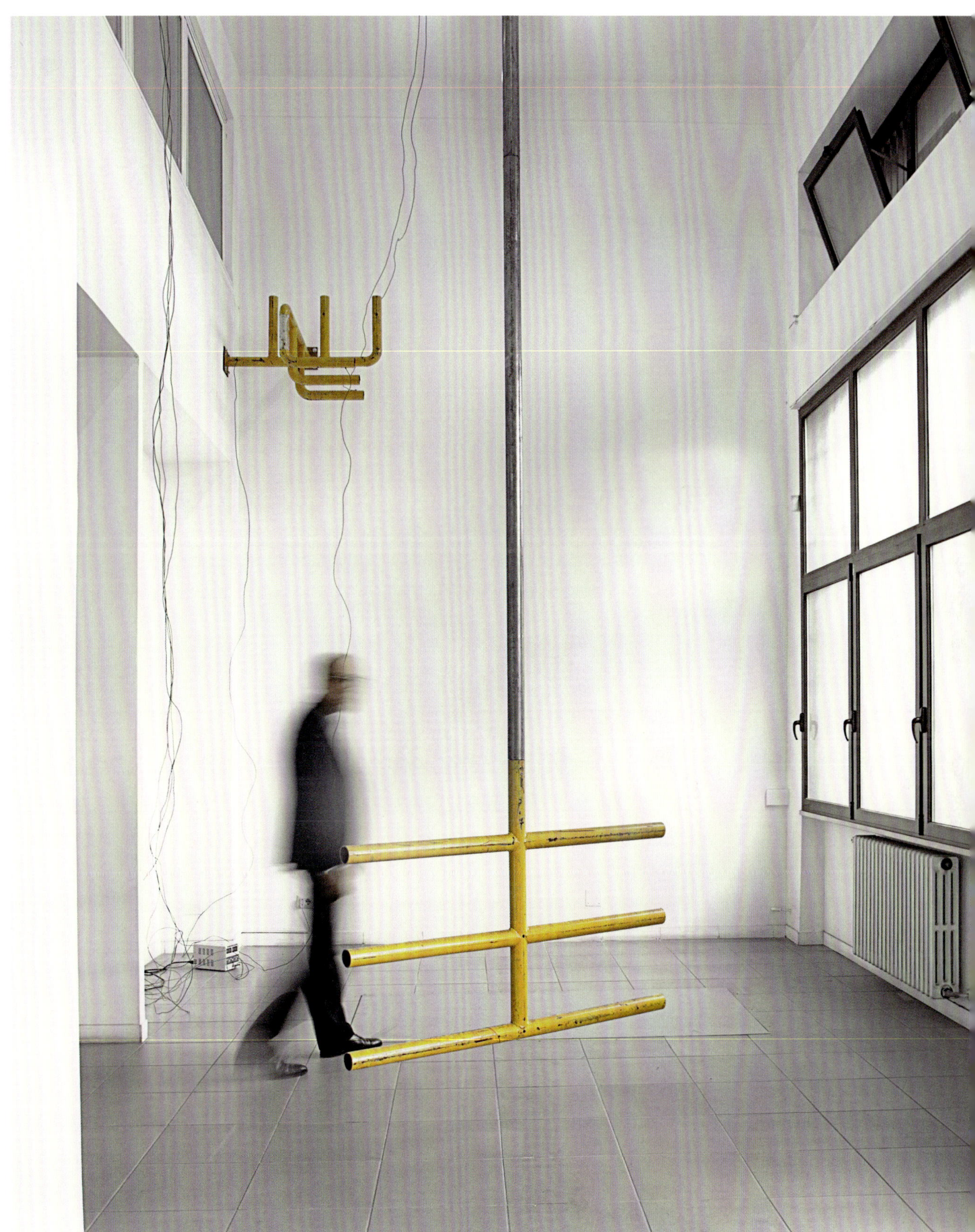

Ground (So You Grab a Piece of Something That You Think Is Going to Last) (2017)
Rammschutz, Stahlrohr, Motor, Netzgerät, Kabel /
fender, steel tube, motor, power supply unit, cable

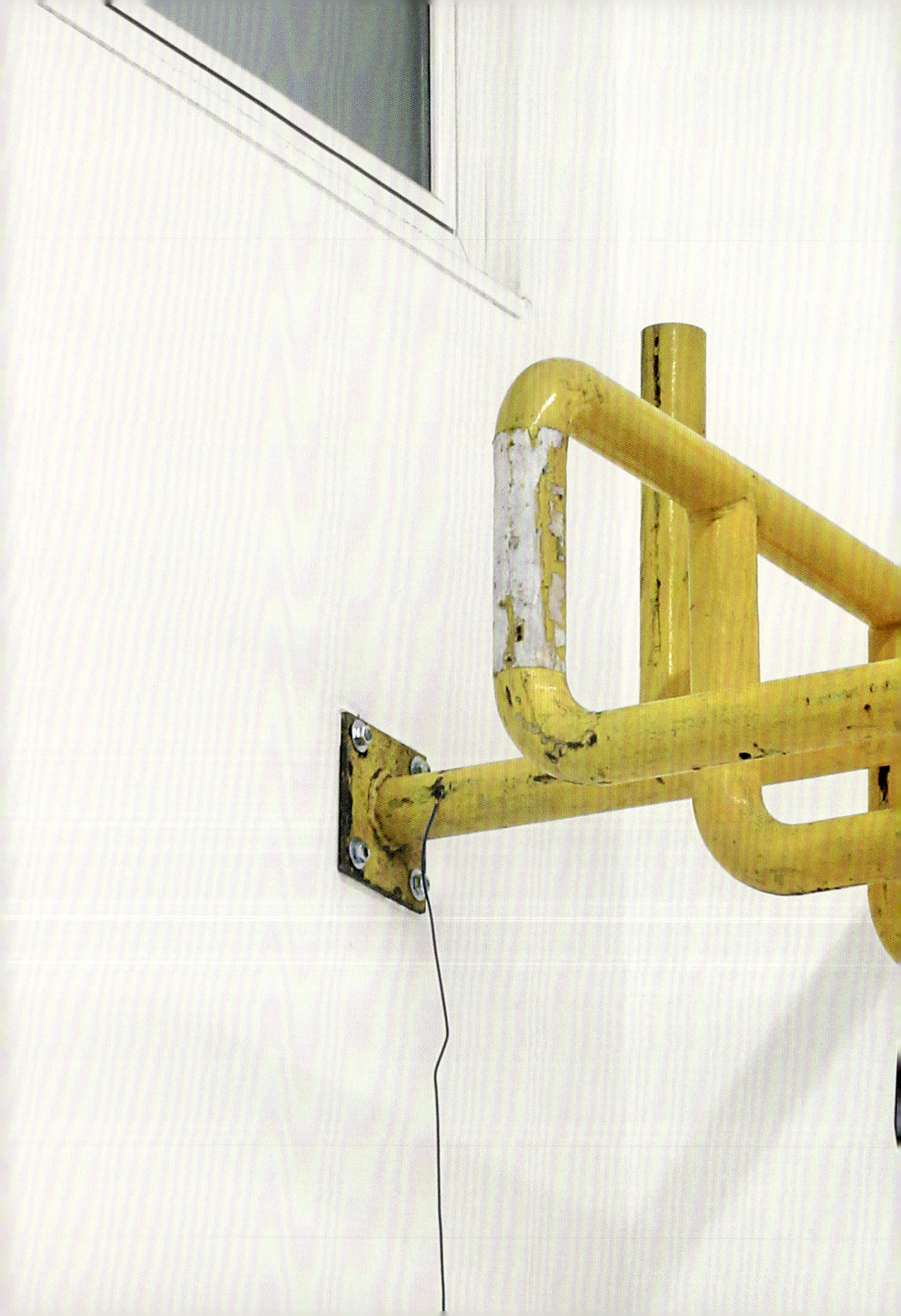

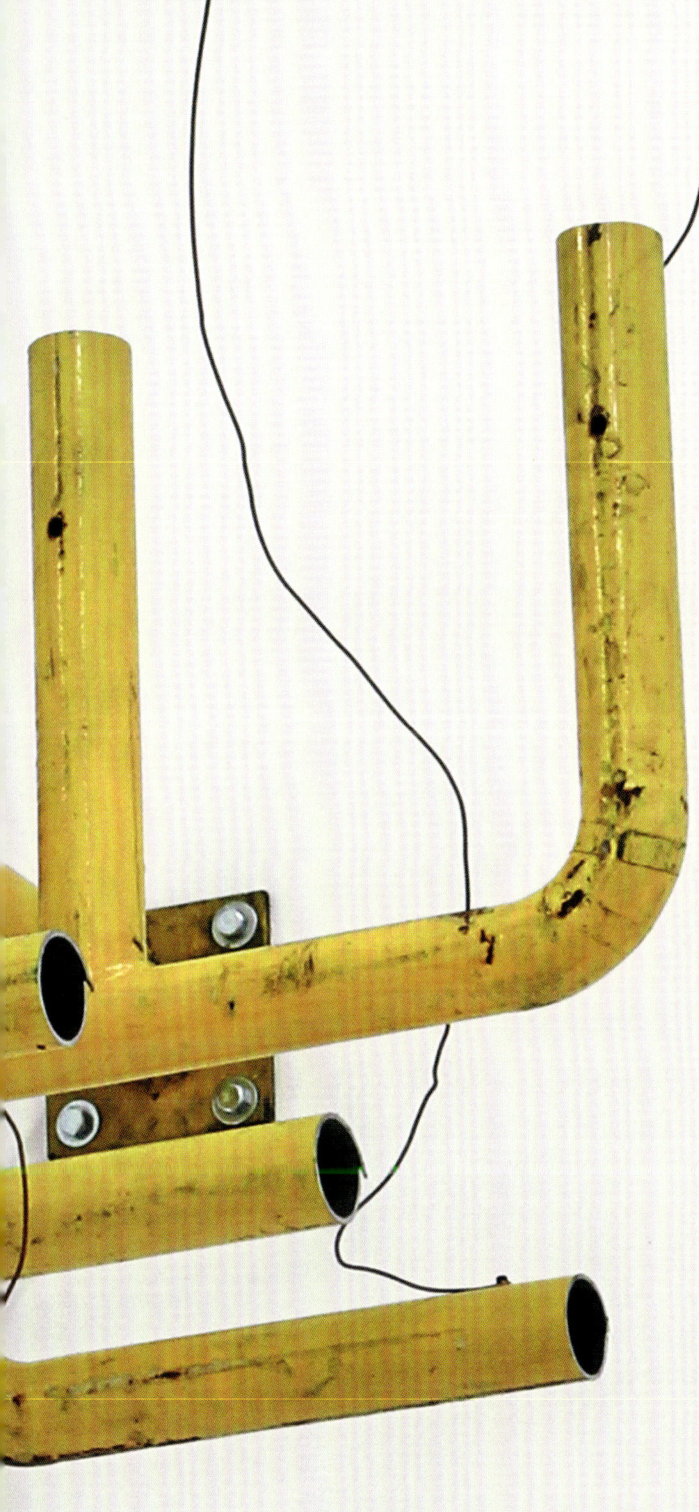

I and it, it and I
Florian Neufeldt und die Frage nach dem Ding

Neben den Hexen, die lange Zeit hinter der Wand meines Kinderzimmers zu Hause waren und sich lediglich des Nachts bemerkbar machten, bewohnte eine weitere Nachtgestalt – oder waren es mehrere? – den Hohlraum oberhalb der hohen, mit Leierschwänzen verzierten Stuckdecke. Dieser unsichtbare Jemand, dieses Etwas, dieses Es krabbelte, polterte, kratzte, hielt inne, kratzte, polterte, krabbelte. Nicht jede und nie die ganze Nacht hindurch bewegte es sich: nach links, nach rechts, vor und zurück, rauf, runter und rundherum. Ein Possum sei es wohl gewesen, sagte meine Mutter, die aus den gleichen Gründen in jungen Jahren zur Decke hin zu horchen begonnen hatte. Bis ich allerdings den Dachboden als eigenständigen, besetzbaren Raum, zumal als tierischen Hort begriffen hatte, verstrichen etliche Jahre. Zunächst einmal war es ja die Decke selbst, die ein Eigenleben zu führen schien, die Geräusche von sich gab und eine Sprache sprach, die ein Ding war, das »dingte«[1].

Jahrzehnte später, auf der anderen Seite der Welt, dingte über meinem Kopf erneut eine Decke, eine schnörkellose, aus Spanplatten zusammenmontierte Fläche, die Florian Neufeldt 2009 in den sonst leeren Raum der Berliner Galerie Opdahl eingezogen hatte. In unregelmäßigen Abständen an scheinbar willkürlichen Stellen wurde diese von oben durchbohrt. Ein feiner Staub muss dabei herabgerieselt sein, wobei ich mich jetzt hauptsächlich an den eindringlichen Zahnarztklang und an die Bewegungen des unnachgiebig bohrenden Etwas erinnere, das sich wie die Possums von einst von hier nach da nach dort begab, um seine wie auch immer geartete Aufgabe zu erfüllen. Vor allem jedoch erinnere ich mich an die Dinghaftigkeit der durchlöcherten Decke, die im Zuge ihrer sich allmählich auflösenden Funktionalität manifest wurde. *I and it, it and I*, so hieß, so heißt die Arbeit.[2]

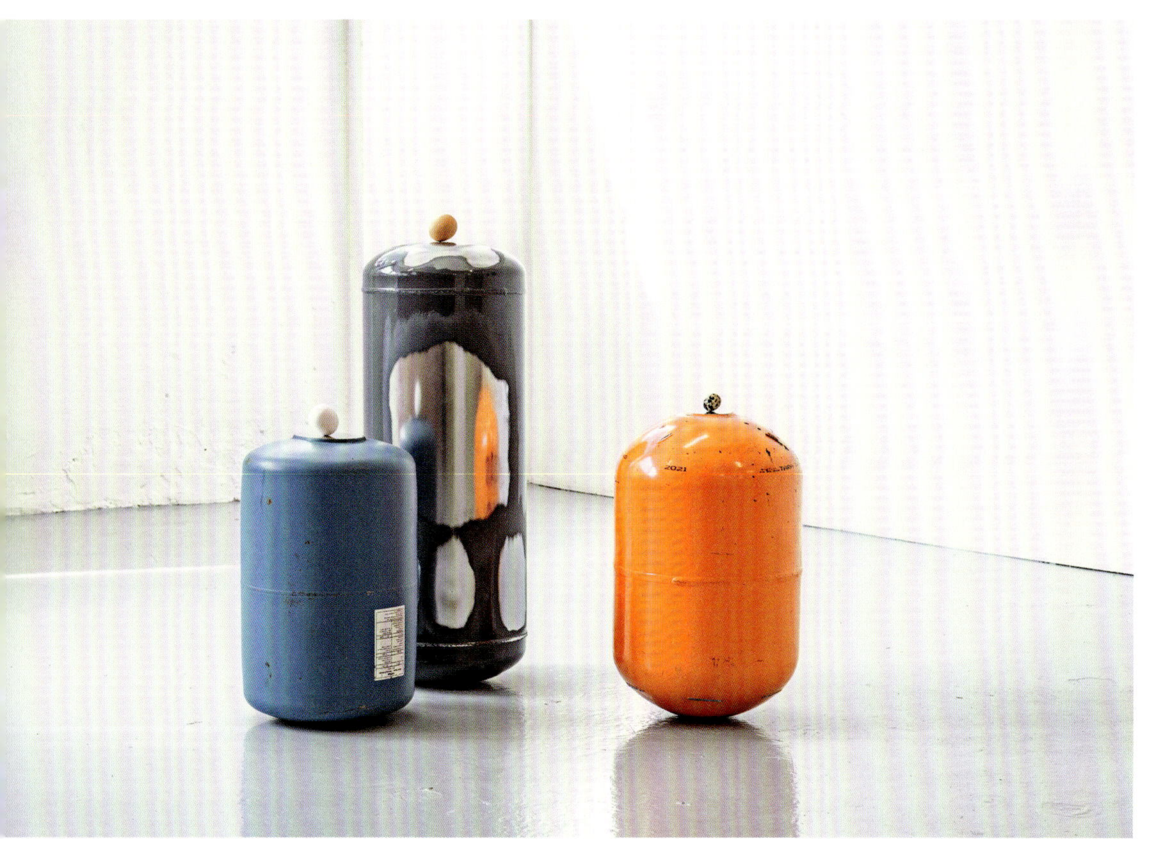

Sealed Vessels (2018)
Gasflaschen, Hühnereier, Wachtelei /
gas bottles, chicken eggs, quail egg

I and it, it and I
Florian Neufeldt and the Question Concerning the Thing

Apart from the witches, who for the longest time resided behind the wall of my childhood bedroom, only making their presence felt at night, there lived another nocturnal figure – or were there several? – in the cavity above the high moulded ceiling featuring lyrebirds and waratahs. This invisible Someone, this Something, this It would scuttle, clatter, scratch, pause a while, scratch, clatter, scuttle. Not every night and never all night long, it would scurry from left to right, forwards and backwards, up, down and around. Most likely it was a possum, or so my mother told me. The very same sounds had taught her as a child to listen closely to ceilings and the realm overhead. Yet many years would pass before I recognised the attic for what it was: an autonomous area, a space that could be occupied, not least by animals in search of shelter. Indeed, for the large part of my childhood the ceiling itself seemed to have a life of its own. It made noises and spoke a language; it was a thing that 'thinged'.[1]

Decades later, on the other side of the world, a ceiling once again 'thinged' above my head. This time the surface was unadorned, assembled by Florian Neufeldt from chipboard panels and installed in an otherwise empty room within Berlin's Galerie Opdahl in 2009. From above, holes were being drilled into the ceiling at irregular intervals in seemingly random places by an invisible creature of sorts. A fine dust must have trickled down through the holes, although now it is more the penetrating sound of the drill I recall, reminiscent of visits to the dentist, and the relentless toing and froing of that Something up above me, which, much like the possum of my childhood, was busily

Was sich bereits im Titel sprachlich ereignet, überträgt sich unmittelbar auf die räumliche Erfahrung: Mensch begegnet Ding, Ding begegnet Mensch. Beide sind verbunden durch ein vielschichtig aufgeladenes, alles irgendwie bedingendes »and«, das die Grenzen zwischen Subjekt und Objekt verwischt. Um diese Konjunktion, die in der Grammatik unseres in der Materie begründeten Alltags eine Schlüsselrolle spielt, scheint sich nicht nur dieses Werk zu drehen, sondern viele, wenn nicht sogar jede Arbeit des Künstlers. Aber wie genau? Mit wem tritt er, mit wem treten seine Werke dabei ins Gespräch? Was gibt es zu bereden?

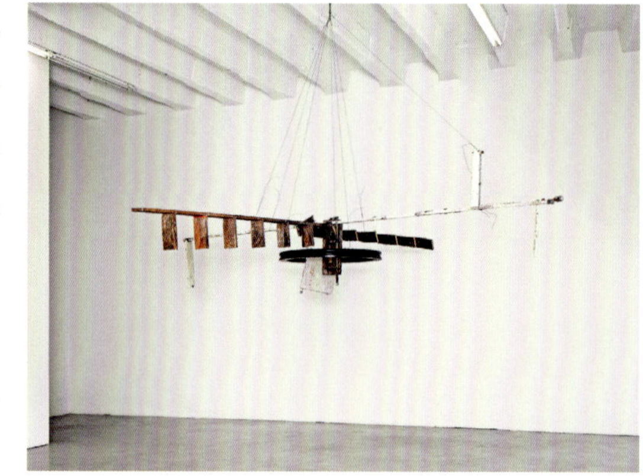

Die Frage nach dem Ding, nach dem Etwas, »was nicht nichts« ist und welches das Menschsein bedingt, ist »schon alt«, wie Martin Heidegger in seiner Vorlesung zur Dingheit der Dinge konstatiert. Das »stets Neue an ihr« sei nur, »daß sie immer wieder gefragt werden muß«.[3] Zwar ändere sich an den Dingen nichts, wenn wir »die Geschichte der Entdeckung und Auslegung der Dingheit des Dinges« zur Kenntnis nehmen. »Die elektrische Straßenbahn fährt deshalb nicht anders wie vordem; die Kreide ist eine Kreide, die Rose eine Rose und die Katze

engaged in some wholly inscrutable task. More than anything else, however, I remember the thinghood of the perforated ceiling, which became increasingly manifest in the course of its gradually disintegrating functionality. The work was, is, called *I and it, it and I*.[2] The linguistic event in the title directly corresponds to what happens in the space: person encounters thing, thing encounters person. Both are bound together by a complex, loaded 'and', which somehow makes everything conditional and blurs the boundaries between subject and object. This conjunction, which plays a key role in the grammar of our everyday material existence, seems to play a pivotal role not only in this work but in many – if not all – of the artist's other works. But how exactly? With whom does he, with whom do his works converse? And what is there to discuss?

The question concerning the thing, the Something 'which is not nothing' that determines what is human, is 'quite old', as Martin Heidegger states in his lecture on

eine Katze«.[4] Und dennoch: Seit den vorsokratischen Überlegungen des griechischen Philosophen Anaximander, für den das Ding weder aus dem Nichts noch im Untergang zu nichts werden kann, steht eine solche Befragung immer wieder auf der Tagesordnung, weil es in seiner Fremdheit »das erste Außen« bildet, so Jacques Lacan, »woran sich der ganze Weg des Subjekts orientiert«.[5] Man denke etwa an Immanuel Kants umwälzendes Postulat eines transzendenten Dinges-an-sich im 18. Jahrhundert oder an die Warentheorie, mit der Karl Marx im darauffolgenden Jahrhundert *Das Kapital* beginnt und die den Gebrauchs- beziehungsweise Tauschwert der Dinge in den Vordergrund stellt.

Im langen 20. Jahrhundert, so Bill Brown in seinen wegweisenden Aufsätzen zur »Thing Theory«, wurde das Ding als Fetisch, Idol, Totem, Phantasma, Mitwirkendes, Ereignis oder Erzählung immer wieder neu gedacht, ob in Übereinstimmung mit, im Widerspruch zu oder schlichtweg jenseits der Logik des Kapitalismus.[6] Welches Jahrzehnt habe sich nicht mit dem Ding auseinandergesetzt? Welche Epoche in ihm nicht ihre zeitspezifischen Wahrheiten zum Wesen des Menschlichen ausfindig machen wollen? In seiner *Philosophie des Geldes* argumentiert etwa Georg Simmel, dass der im empirischen Leben vor uns stehende fertige Gegenstand

A Shot in the Dark (II) (2011)
Leitern, MDF, Lack, Draht /
ladders, MDF, varnish, wire
57 × 350 × 340 cm

the thingness of things. What 'remains ever new' is merely that the question 'must be asked again and again'.[3] Indeed, nothing changes in things if we acknowledge 'the history of the disclosure and interpretation of thingness of the thing': 'the streetcar goes no differently than before, the chalk is a chalk, the rose is a rose, the cat is a cat'.[4] And yet: since the pre-Socratic reflections of the Greek philosopher Anaximander, for whom the thing can neither come from nothing nor become nothing in its demise, such questioning has ever and again appeared on the agenda. This is because, in its otherness, the thing forms what Jacques Lacan calls the 'first exterior [...] around which the entire progression of the subject orients itself'.[5] We may recall, for example, Immanuel Kant's groundbreaking postulate of a transcendental thing-in-itself in the eighteenth century or the commodity theory with which Karl Marx began *Das Kapital* in the following century with its emphasis on the use value or exchange value of things.

erst zum »Ding« werde, indem wir ihn begehren.[7] Für Walter Benjamin wiederum ist es die Sprache, die zur Dingwerdung des Dings wesentlich beiträgt: »Weder in der belebten noch in der unbelebten Natur«, schreibt er in »Über Sprache überhaupt und über die Sprache des Menschen«, gebe es ein Ding, das »nicht in gewisser Weise an der Sprache teilhätte«, denn es sei »jedem wesentlich, seinen geistigen Inhalt mitzuteilen«.[8] Dass in einer auf Warentausch beruhenden Gesellschaft alles – selbst ein Mensch, ein Gedanke, ein Gefühl, ein Bewusstsein – zum Ding werden beziehungsweise sich zum Ding machen kann, untersucht Georg Lukács in »Die Verdinglichung und das Bewusstsein des Proletariats«[9]. Inwiefern eine solche »Liebe zu den Dingen«[10] der sozialen Freiheit zugrunde liegt, wie Georg Wilhelm Friedrich Hegel in seiner Jenaer Vorlesung zur *Philosophie des Geistes* (1805/06)[11] und später Theodor W. Adorno in seiner *Negativen Dialektik* suggerieren, oder vielmehr der Unfreiheit, so Lukács,[12] sei hier dahingestellt.

Für Martin Heidegger wie für Jacques Lacan, für Bill Brown wie für Jacques Derrida[13] sind Dinge im Gegensatz zu den Objekten, denen sie innewohnen, stets im Prozess begriffen. Sie sind mystisch, verborgen, zum Erscheinen zu bringen, was letztlich nur dann gelingen kann, so Brown,

In the long twentieth century, as Bill Brown details in his pioneering essays on 'Thing Theory', the thing has been reconceptualised countless times as fetish, idol, totem, spectre, participant, event or narrative, whether in keeping or in conflict with – or indeed simply beyond – the logic of capitalism.[6] Which decade has not addressed the issue of the thing? Which epoch has not looked to the thing in its quest to discover time-specific truths on the essence of what it means to be human? In *The Philosophy of Money*, Georg Simmel argues, for example, that the finished object that stands before us in empirical life only becomes a 'thing' at the point at which we desire it.[7] For Walter Benjamin, on the other hand, it is language that contributes primarily to the 'becoming-thing' of the thing. In his essay 'On Language as Such and the Language of Man', he writes that there is 'no event or thing in either animate or inanimate nature that does not in some way partake of language, for it is in the nature of all to communicate their mental

wenn ein Objekt aus dem Kontext gerissen wird oder aufhört zu funktionieren, wenn etwa ein Fenster so schmutzig ist, dass man nicht mehr durch das Glas hindurchschauen kann, wenn ein Automotor abgewürgt wird oder eine Bohrmaschine kaputtgeht.[14] Nach der Auffassung Tim Ingolds sind Dinge »Ansammlungen von in Bewegung befindlichen Materialien«, die wir berühren oder beobachten, indem wir »die Bewegungen unseres eigenen Seins (oder vielmehr Werdens) in Übereinstimmung mit den Bewegungen der Materialien« bringen.[15] Als solche haben sie eine ihnen eigene Geschichtlichkeit.[16]

Alphonso Lingis zufolge sind Dinge vor allem sinnlich und affektiv: Sie ziehen uns an, lenken unsere Aufmerksamkeit auf sich, rufen bestimmte Gefühlslagen hervor. Sie unterstützen, ernähren und versorgen uns, sie betören und entzücken uns, sie regen uns an oder schwächen uns. Sie veranlassen uns, unsere Kräfte mit den ihren zu verbinden.[17] Geht man wie etwa Bruno Latour oder Jane Bennett von Dingen als handelnden und sprechenden Entitäten aus, als »Quasiobjekten«, die, mit Michel Serres, zugleich Subjekte sein können beziehungsweise »Quasisubjekte«, die zugleich Objekte sein können,[18] so dürften sie zudem als

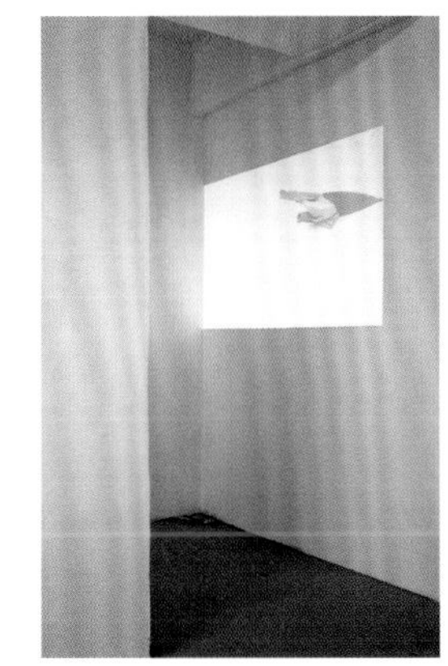

Of Fingers and Buttons (2009)
Videoprojektion / video projection
16:9 (Loop / loop), 4:32 min

meanings'.[8] How everything – a person, a thought, a feeling, a consciousness – can become a thing or make a thing of itself in a society based on the exchange of commodities is explored by Georg Lukács in his essay 'Reification and the Consciousness of the Proletariat'.[9] Whether such a 'love of things', per Theodor W. Adorno in his *Negative Dialectics*, might form the foundation of social freedom,[10] as Georg Wilhelm Friedrich Hegel also argues in his *Jena Lectures on the Philosophy of Spirit*,[11] or rather pave the way to a state of 'unfreedom' as Lukács would have it,[12] remains an open question.

For Martin Heidegger and Jacques Lacan, for Bill Brown and Jacques Derrida,[13] things, in contrast to the objects to which they are intrinsic, are constantly in a state of becoming. They are mystical, hidden, to be brought to the fore. According to Brown, this can ultimately only happen when an object is wrested from its context or when it stops working for us, for example when a window gets so dirty that we cannot see

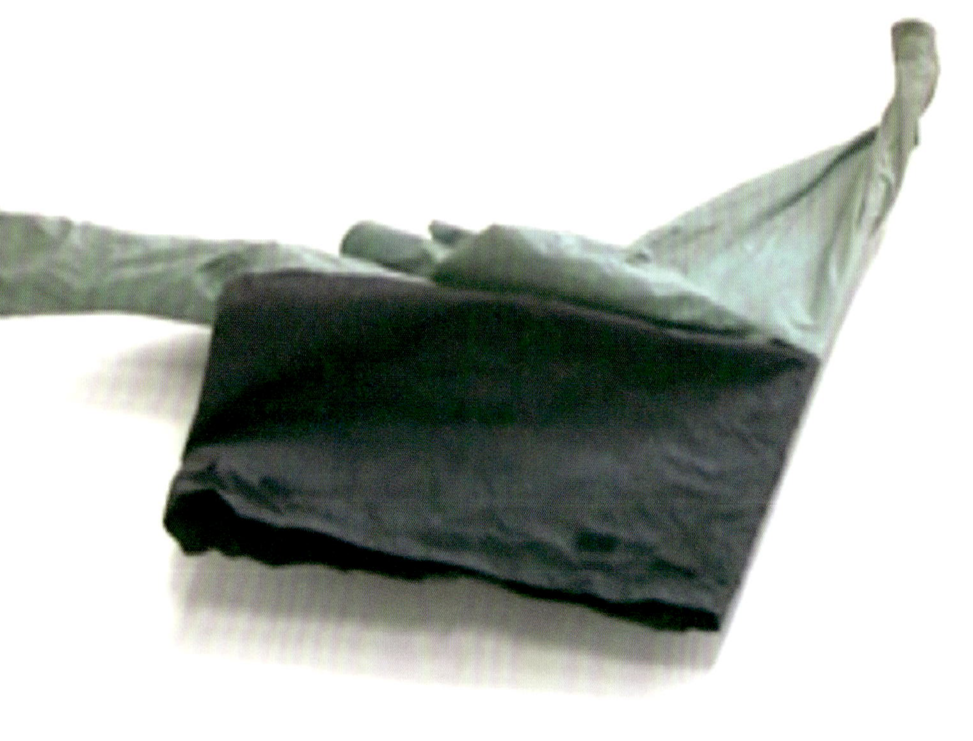

Of Fingers and Buttons (2009)
Videoprojektion / video projection
16:9 (Loop / loop), 4:32 min

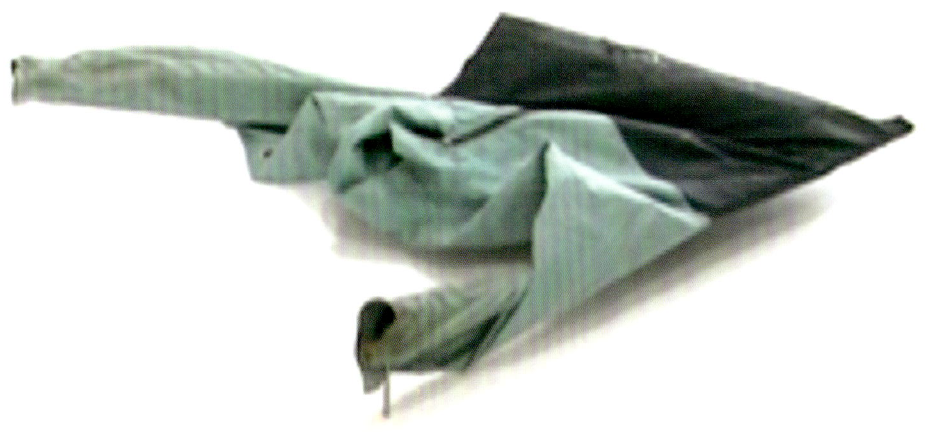

Hoffnungsträger einer emanzipatorischen Politik des Überlebens zu verstehen sein, einer Politik, die neben dem Menschen Tiere, Pflanzen, Luft, Wasser sowie technische Objekte berücksichtigt und so den Subjekt-Objekt-Dualismus zur Disposition stellt, in dem der menschliche Exzeptionalismus begründet wird.[19] An diesem zunehmend brisanten Diskurs um unsere Verschränkung mit der Dingwelt, um unsere Kohabitation und Kooperation mit den darin dingenden Dingen beteiligt sich Florian Neufeldt in seiner künstlerischen Arbeit. Als teile er die Skepsis von Gertrude Stein gegenüber Substantiven und Adjektiven, stellt er Verdichtungen von Verben und Adverbien, Präpositionen und Konjunktionen eher als in sich ruhende Substantive in den Raum. Denn Verben und Adverbien haben, so Stein, »eine sehr hübsche Eigenschaft und das ist daß sie so falsch sein können. [...] Außer imstande zu sein sich zu irren und Fehler zu machen, können Verben sich verändern um auszusehen wie sie selbst oder um auszusehen wie etwas anderes, sie sind, sozusagen in Bewegung und Adverbien bewegen sich mit ihnen«.[20] *I and it, it and I.* Kein Ich ohne Es. Kein Es ohne Ich. Ein kreisendes, eindringliches, zunehmendes Nachdenken ist es, das man spürt, wenn man die Objekte, die sich entfaltenden Räume, die offenen Situationen erlebt, die der Künstler schafft beziehungsweise entstehen lässt. Ein oftmals beklemmendes, mal im Nacken sitzendes, gelegentlich ironisches Nachdenken über das Ding, über die Dingheit der Dinge ist es, das stets von den Dingen selbst ausgeht: Decken, Böden, Wände und Fenster, Türen und Türzargen, Stühle, Tische, Heizkörper, Lampen, Kisten, Gasflaschen, Neonröhren, Strom, Stimmen, Sprichwörter, Worte. Es sind meist vorgefundene, auf ihre Art sprechende, im Werden begriffene Entitäten, die der Künstler in seinem Gedankenprozess ergreift, die er verwandelt, verfremdet, versetzt oder neu verbindet, die er faltet,

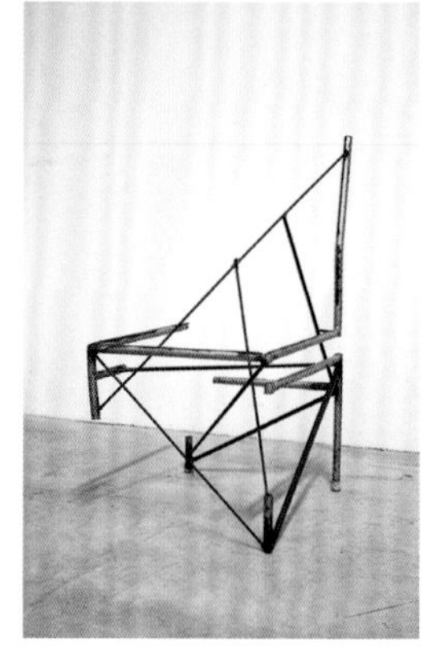

Statiker (2013)
Stuhlgestell, Stahl / chair frame, steel
85 × 40 × 46 cm

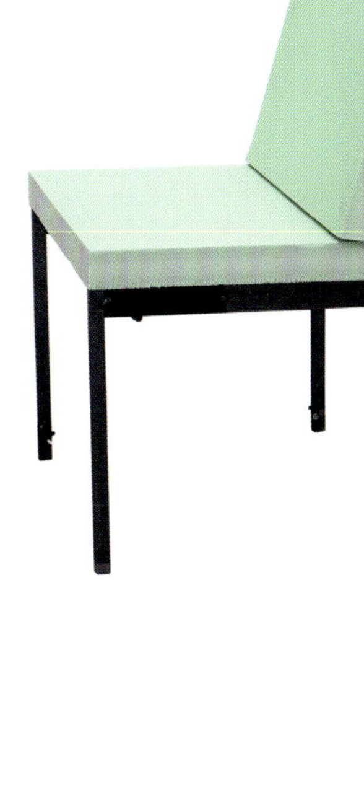

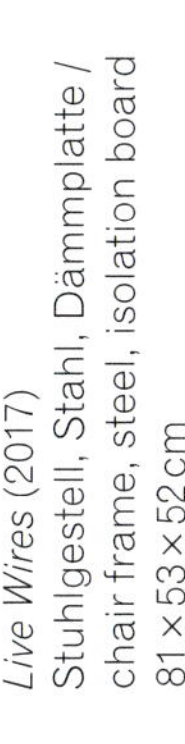

Live Wires (2017)
Stuhlgestell, Stahl, Dämmplatte / chair frame, steel, isolation board
81 × 53 × 52 cm

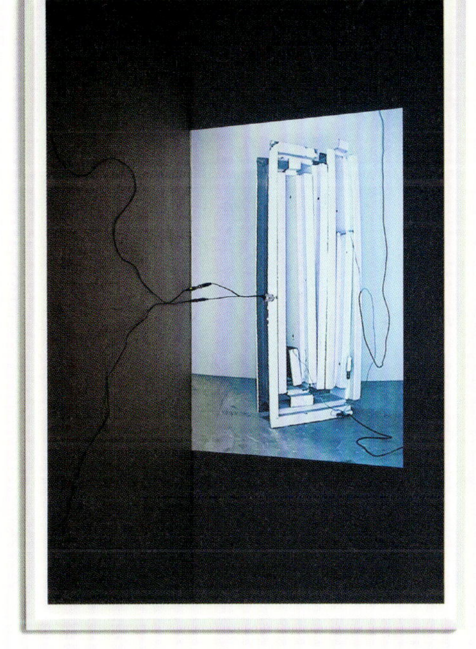

Live Wires (Conducting Blue) (2015)
Inkjet Print, gerahmt hinter Glas / inkjet print, framed behind glass
85 × 59,5 cm

through the glass, when a car stalls or a drill breaks.[14] Tim Ingold is of the view that things are 'gatherings of materials in motion' that we touch or observe by bringing 'the movements of our own being (or rather, becoming) into correspondence with the movements of the materials'.[15] As such, they have their own inherent historicity.[16]

Alphonso Lingis suggests that things are primarily sensuous and affective: they lure us, provoke us, direct us, thereby evoking certain emotional states. They support, nourish and sustain us, they beguile and delight, stimulate or weaken us. They motivate us to join forces with them.[17] If, like Bruno Latour or Jane Bennett, we assume that things are active and meaningful entities, 'quasi-objects', which, according to Michael Serres can also be subjects or 'quasi-subjects' that in turn can also be objects,[18] we might find in them some hope for an emancipatory policy of survival. It would be a policy that is mindful of humans, but also takes into consideration animals, plants, air, water and technical objects, thereby contesting the subject-object dualism at the core of human exceptionalism.[19]

In his artistic practice Florian Neufeldt participates in this increasingly controversial debate on our entanglement with the thing world, on our cohabitation and cooperation with the thinging things therein. As though he shared Gertrude Stein's scepticism about nouns and adjectives, his works are more likely to embody verbs and adverbs, prepositions and conjunctions than static nouns.

schneidet, abschleift, bricht, verschließt, unter Strom oder in Bewegung setzt, ohne jemals ganz die Spur zurück zum Gewesenen verwischen zu wollen.
Dabei sind es weniger die Materialien an sich, für die sich Neufeldt interessiert: Nicht irgendeine Metallplatte oder Glasscheibe, nicht irgendein Stück Holz, Styropor oder Pappe fesselt ihn, spricht mit ihm, will allein aufgrund ihrer oder seiner Beschaffenheit bildhauerisch erkundet werden. Vielmehr sind es die in den menschlichen Alltag inbegriffenen und so gesellschaftlich aufgeladenen Objekte, die seine Aufmerksamkeit auf sich lenken, Gebrauchsgegenstände, die uns zu überraschen und zu affizieren vermögen, denen eine Geschichte innewohnt, die auszuloten, weiter- oder anders zu erzählen wäre. Es sind unspektakuläre, vielfach sperrige, sich im unmittelbaren Umfeld des Künstlers befindliche Dinge, die ein Innenleben – eine Seele? – zu haben, ja etwas in sich zu bergen scheinen, an das dekonstruktiv rekonstruktiv anzunähern sich lohnt: eine Wand, die einen Doppelgänger hat,[21] ein Heizkörper, der seiner Temperatur vergewissert werden möchte,[22] ein fragil daherkommendes, vor sich hin balancierendes Stuhlgestell,[23] ein mit sich selbst sprechendes Tischgestell,[24] ein so zusammengefalteter Türrahmen, dass ihn keiner mit einer Schwelle, mit einem Ein- oder Austritt

o. T. / Untitled (1998)
Schaumstoffmatratze /
foam matress

For verbs and adverbs, as Stein contends, have 'one very nice quality and that is that they can be so mistaken. [...] Beside being able to be mistaken and to make mistakes verbs can change to look like themselves or to look like something else, they are, so to speak on the move and adverbs move with them.'[20] *I and it, it and I*. No I without it. No it without I. It is a circling, insistent, burgeoning thought process that we see set in motion by the objects, the unfolding spaces, the open situations the artist creates or allows to evolve. It is an often claustrophobic, at times oppressive, even occasionally ironic contemplation of the thing, of the thingness of things, that invariably takes as its point of departure the things themselves: ceilings, floors, walls and windows, doors and doorframes, chairs, tables, heaters, lamps, boxes, gas cylinders, fluorescent tubes, electricity, voices, sayings, words. They are mostly entities that have been found, that are in the process of becoming, and that speak a language all of their

verwechseln kann,[25] eine zu einem mit Beton verschlossenen Dreiecksprisma geformte, wie der Ouroboros sich selbst in alle Ewigkeit verzehrende Treppe, die niemanden mehr nach oben oder nach unten bringen wird. Purgatorium.[26]
Unten. Unten am Boden stand längere Zeit in Florian Neufeldts Ateliergebäude eine Gasflasche herum, aus der die 2018 entstandene Arbeit *Sealed Vessels*[27] hervorging. Eines Tages machte die Flasche auf sich, auf ihr Gefäßsein aufmerksam, darauf, dass sie innen etwas aufbewahrt beziehungsweise aufbewahrte, das nach außen gelangen soll. Das auf einmal zum Ding gewordene Objekt entledigte der Künstler seiner Funktion, indem er die Flasche für immer verschloss: Er entfernte das Ventil und schweißte die Öffnung zu. Weitere unterschiedlich anmutende Gasflaschen – klein, groß, rundlich, schlank, orange, rot, grün, blau – unterzog er der gleichen Prozedur. Im Zuge der Umformung verwandelten sich die nunmehr hermetisch abgeschlossenen Gefäße mit ihrem diffusen, anwesend und nicht seienden Inhalt in der Wahrnehmung des Künstlers in Sockel. Sockel wofür? Für das Urgefäß, das Ei, ein ebenfalls im Atelier herumliegendes Ding, das bei aller symbolischen

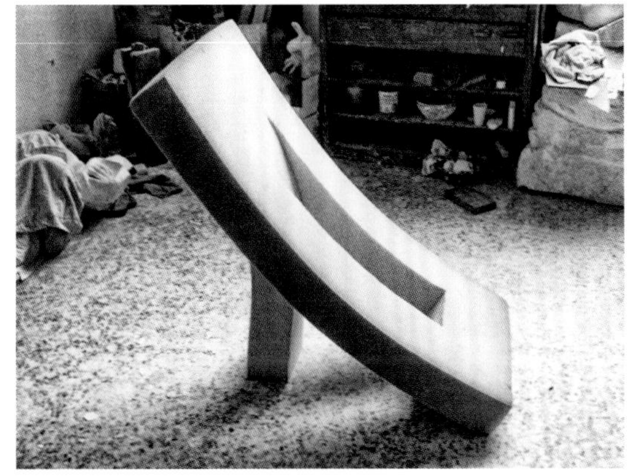

own. The artist incorporates them into his thought process and proceeds to transform, alienate, displace or reconfigure them, to fold, cut, abrade or polish, break or seal them, to charge them with electricity or set them in motion. This he does without ever seeking to entirely erase the trace of what has been.
And yet, it is not so much the material itself that interests Neufeldt: it is not some sheet of metal or pane of glass, not some piece of wood, polystyrene or cardboard that captivates him, that speaks to him, or whose properties he is keen to mine for their sculptural potential. On the contrary, he is drawn to objects very much entrenched in everyday life, to socially charged, utilitarian objects that may surprise, touch or affect us, objects that have a history to be interrogated, continued or retold. They are unspectacular, frequently awkward things that the artist typically encounters within his immediate surroundings, things that appear to have an inner life – dare one say

Überfrachtung zunächst aufgrund seiner Form wie seines Verhaltens ins Auge fiel. Denn das im Laufe des Herumliegens komplett ausgetrocknete Ei lag nicht erwartungsgemäß ganz auf der Seite, sondern strebte mit einem Ende nach oben, der Schwerkraft zum Trotz schräg balancierend: zwei entfremdete Gefäße unsicheren Inhalts, einander so gegenübergestellt, dass sie nicht nur auf das ewige, seit Auguste Rodin besonders umstrittene Sockelproblem verweisen – wo fängt eine Skulptur an und wo hört sie auf? Sondern zugleich fassen die uns verborgen bleibenden Innenräume die für den Künstler viel wesentlichere Frage nach der Dingheit der beiden miteinander sprechenden Körper – Gasflasche und Ei – wie des Gefäßes schlechthin, des Dinges, des »It«, ohne das – wie oben erläutert – es kein »I«, kein »Ich« gäbe.

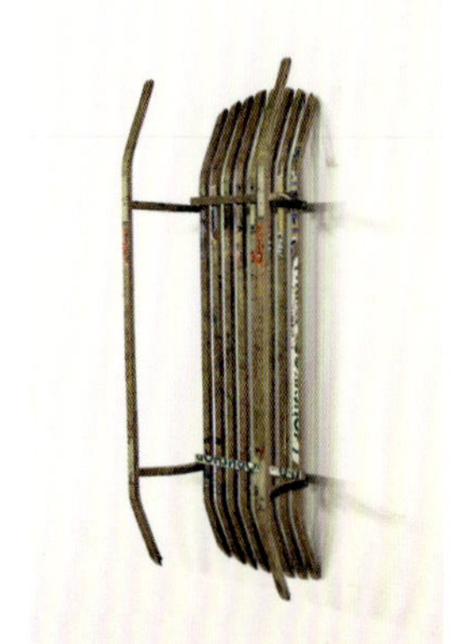

Rosebud (2006/11)
Skateboard-Deck / skateboard deck
35 × 75 × 25 cm

Rosalind Krauss begreift Bildhauerei als Medium, das »an der Schnittstelle von Stillstand und Bewegung, von angehaltener und vergehender Zeit«[28] verortet ist – damit umreißt sie die bei dieser Kunstform wohl am schwersten zu ergründende Dingheit eines Dings am schärfsten. Und das zeigen uns die Arbeiten – und das Arbeiten – von Florian Neufeldt. Ohne theoretischen Überbau, ohne politisches Programm, ohne das Bedürfnis, eine nichtanthropozentrische Welt zu postulieren oder eine wie auch immer geartete Emanzipation herbeizuführen, stellen die dingenden Dinge von Neufeldt die Frage nach dem Ding immer neu. In Abwesenheit eines nächtlich hierhin und dahin huschenden Possums im Dach und überhaupt erinnert Neufeldts ebenso unnachgiebige wie vielgestaltige Reartikulation dieses zentralen ontologischen Problems daran, dass wir mit den Dingen, den »gleich nahen und gleich fernen Anwesenden«[29], nie fertig werden.

soul? – indeed, that seem to contain something worth getting to the bottom of in a manner as deconstructive as it is reconstructive: a wall with a doppelgänger;[21] a heater eager to be reassured of its temperature;[22] a fragile chair frame caught in a seemingly precarious balancing act;[23] a table frame that talks to itself;[24] a doorframe folded in such a way as to preclude its ever being mistaken for a threshold, an entrance or an exit;[25] a set of steps folded to form a triangular prism sealed with concrete, an eternally twisting body, which, redolent of the self-devouring ouroboros, will never again convey anybody up or down – purgatory.[26]

Look down. Down on the ground. A gas cylinder left lying around in the building where Florian Neufeldt's studio is located gave rise to his 2018 work, *Sealed Vessels*.[27] One day, the cylinder spoke to him out of the blue, drew attention to itself, to its status as a vessel, to the fact that it stores – or once stored – within it something intended for release. The object, having at that moment become a thing, was subsequently divested of its function by the artist. Removing the valve and welding the opening closed, he permanently sealed the cylinder. From there he went on to manipulate all manner of other gas cylinders – small, large, round, slim, orange, red, green, blue – in the same way. In their transformed state the now hermetically sealed vessels, with their diffuse, at once present and absent contents, reminded the artist of pedestals. Pedestals for what? For the primordial vessel, the egg, another thing the artist found coincidentally in his studio. For all its symbolic overtones, however, it was the form and behaviour of the egg that caught the artist's eye. Having been left lying around for so long that it had completely dried out, the egg did not lie entirely on its side as would be expected. Instead, in defiance of gravity, one end of the egg was pointing upwards, making it appear to balance at an angle. In placing the egg on the gas cylinder, Neufeldt juxtaposed two differently alienated vessels of uncertain contents in such a way as to evoke, on the one hand, the perpetual art-historical problem of the pedestal, particularly virulent since the time of Auguste Rodin, namely: where does a sculpture begin and where does it end? On the other hand, the forever concealed interiors of the two vessels raised what the artist considered the far more pertinent question concerning the thingness of the two interacting bodies – gas cylinder and egg – as indeed of the vessel in its own right, of the thing, of the 'it', without which, as discussed above, there would be no 'I'.

Rosalind Krauss sees sculpture as a medium 'located at the juncture between stillness and motion, time arrested and time passing'.[28] She thus astutely adumbrates the difficulty of grasping the thingness of a thing, perhaps in this medium more than any other. Florian Neufeldt's works – and practice – offer us an incisive insight into this very topos. Without a theoretical superstructure, without a political agenda, without the need to posit a non-anthropocentric world or to precipitate some kind of emancipation, Neufeldt's 'thinging things' assiduously pose the 'question concerning the thing' from ever-shifting perspectives. With or without possums up in the roof, scurrying here and there in the night, Neufeldt's relentless rearticulation of this key ontological problem reminds us of the fact that we can never be finished with those 'equally near and equally far' presences we call things.[29]

Anmerkungen

1 Martin Heidegger, »Das Ding« [1950], in: ders., Gesamtausgabe, 1. Abteilung: *Veröffentlichte Schriften 1910–1976*, Bd. 7: *Vorträge und Aufsätze*, Frankfurt am Main 2000, S. 165–187, hier S. 175.
2 *I and it, it and I*, 2009, Abb. S. 60–63.
3 Martin Heidegger, *Die Frage nach dem Ding. Zu Kants Lehre von den transzendentalen Grundsätzen* [1935/36], Gesamtausgabe, 2. Abteilung: *Vorlesungen 1923–1944*, Bd. 41, Frankfurt am Main 1984, S. 1, §1, S. 5f., §2.
4 Ebd., S. 39, §10.
5 Jacques Lacan, *Die Ethik der Psychoanalyse: Das Seminar, Buch 7 (1959–1960)*, hg. von Norbert Haas und Hans-Joachim Metzger, übers. von Norbert Haas, Weinheim und Berlin 1996, S. 146.
6 Vgl. etwa Bill Brown, »Thing Theory«, in: *Critical Inquiry*, Bd. 28, Heft 1 (Herbst 2001), S. 1–22, hier S. 13ff.; ders., *A Sense of Things. The Object Matter of American Literature*, Chicago und London 2003; ders., *Other Things*, Chicago und London 2015.
7 Georg Simmel, *Die Philosophie des Geldes* [1900], 5. Auflage, München und Leipzig 1930, S. 12ff.
8 Walter Benjamin, »Über Sprache überhaupt und über die Sprache des Menschen« [1916], in: ders., *Gesammelte Schriften*, Bd. II. 1, Frankfurt am Main 1972, S. 140–156, hier S. 140.
9 Georg Lukács, »Die Verdinglichung und das Bewusstsein des Proletariats« [1923], in ders., *Geschichte und Klassenbewusstsein. Studien über marxistische Dialektik*, Darmstadt und Neuwied 1976, S. 97–192.
10 Theodor W. Adorno zur »Objektivität und Verdinglichung«, in: ders., *Negative Dialektik*, Frankfurt am Main 1966, S. 189.
11 Vgl. Dirk Quadflieg, »Sich zum Ding machen. Hegel und die Grundlagen sozialer Freiheit«, in: ders., *Vom Geist der Sache. Zur Kritik der Verdinglichung*, Frankfurt am Main 2019, S. 99–196.
12 Lukács 1923 (wie Anm. 9), S. 100–104.
13 Vgl. etwa Jacques Derrida, *Falschgeld. Zeit geben 1* [1991], übers. von Andreas Knop und Michael Wetzel, München 1993, S. 58 f. und ders., *Marx' Gespenster* [1993], übers. von Susanne Lüdemann, Frankfurt am Main 1995, S. 203–211.
14 Brown 2001 (wie Anm. 6), S. 4.
15 Tim Ingold, »Ein Fels ist ein Fels ist ein Fels. Eine Ökologie der Materialien«, in: Kerstin Stakemeier und Susanne Witzgall (Hg.), *Macht des Materials – Politik der Materialität*, Zürich und Berlin 2014, S. 65–73, online unter https://www.diaphanes.de/titel/ein-fels-ist-ein-fels-ist-ein-fels-2724 (letzter Zugang: 25. April 2019).
16 Vgl. hierzu Karen Barad, *Agentieller Realismus. Über die Bedeutung materiell-diskursiver Praktiken* [2003/07], übers. von Jürgen Schröder, Frankfurt am Main 2012.
17 Alphonso Lingis, *The Imperative*, Bloomington und Indianapolis 1998, S. 76, 82, 121.
18 Michel Serres, *Der Parasit* [1980], übers. von Michael Bischoff, Frankfurt am Main 1987, S. 345ff.
19 Vgl. etwa Bruno Latour, *Wir sind nie modern gewesen. Versuch einer symmetrischen Anthropologie* [1991], übers. von Gustav Roßler, Frankfurt am Main 2008; Jane Bennett, *Vibrant Matter. A Political Ecology of Things*, Durham und London 2009.
20 Gertrude Stein, »Poetik und Grammatik«, in: dies., *Was ist englische Literatur und andere Vorlesungen in Amerika* [1935], übers. von Marie-Anne Stiebel, Zürich 1965, S. 157–190, hier S. 160.
21 *Doppelgänger (Walls With Flaws)*, 2013, Abb. S. 14–16.
22 *Reassuring a Heater of Its Temperature*, 2014, Abb. S. 52–54.
23 *Statiker*, 2013, Abb. S. 98.
24 *Selbstgespräche (gelb)*, 2016, Abb. S. 27.
25 *Rahmen*, 2018, Abb. S. 22–26.
26 *Treppe*, 2011, Abb. S. 111.
27 *Sealed Vessels*, 2018, Abb. S. 18–21, 91.
28 Rosalind E. Krauss, *Passages in Modern Sculpture*, New York 1977, S. 5.
29 Heidegger 1950 (wie Anm. 1), S. 179.

Notes

1 Martin Heidegger, 'The Thing' [1950], in *Poetry, Language, Thought*, trans. Albert Hofstader (New York: Harper and Row, 1971), pp. 163–180, here p. 172.

2 *I and it, it and I*, 2009, Fig. pp. 60–63.

3 Martin Heidegger, *What Is a Thing*, trans. W . B . Barton, Jr. and Vera Deutsch (Chicago: Henry Regnery Co., 1967), pp. 1, 5.

4 Ibid., p. 41.

5 Jacques Lacan, *The Ethics of Psychoanalysis: 1959–1960: The seminar of Jacques Lacan*, ed. Jacques-Alain Miller, trans. Dennis Porter (London and New York: W. W. Norton & Company, 1997), p. 52.

6 See Bill Brown, 'Thing Theory', in *Critical Inquiry* 28, no. 1 (Autumn 2001): pp. 1–22, here p. 13 ff.; Bill Brown, *A Sense of Things: The Object Matter of American Literature* (Chicago: University of Chicago Press, 2003); Bill Brown, *Other Things* (Chicago: University of Chicago Press, 2015).

7 Georg Simmel, *The Philosophy of Money* [1900], ed. David Frisby, trans. Tom Bottomore and David Frisby (London: Routledge, 2004).

8 Walter Benjamin, 'On Language as Such and the Language of Man' [1916], in *Early Writings, 1910–1917*, trans. Howard Eiland and others (Cambridge: The Belknap Press of Harvard University Press, 2011), pp. 251–269, here p. 251.

9 Georg Lukács, 'Reification and the Consciousness of the Proletariat' [1923], in *History and Class Consciousness: Studies in Marxist Dialectics*, trans. Rodney Livingstone (Cambridge: The MIT Press, 1971), pp. 83–222.

10 Theodor W. Adorno on 'Objectivity and Reification' [1966], in *Negative Dialectics*, trans. E. B. Ashton (New York: Seabury, 1973), pp. 189–192.

11 See Dirk Quadflieg, 'Sich zum Ding machen: Hegel und die Grundlagen sozialer Freiheit', in *Vom Geist der Sache: Zur Kritik der Verdinglichung* (Frankfurt/Main: Campus Verlag, 2019), pp. 99–196.

12 Lukàcs, 1923 (see note 9), pp. 91–92.

13 See, for example, Jacques Derrida, *Given Time: 1. Counterfeit Money* [1991], trans. Peggy Kamuf (Chicago and London: The University of Chicago Press, 1992), pp. 40–41; *Specters of Marx* [1993], trans. Peggy Kamuf (New York and London: Routledge, 1994), pp. 187–193.

14 Brown, 2001 (see note 6), p. 4.

15 Tim Ingold, 'A rock is a rock is a rock: An Ecology of Materials', in Kerstin Stakemeier and Susanne Witzgall (eds.), *Power of Material/ Politics of Materiality* (Zurich: Diaphanes, 2018), pp. 59–65, online at https://www.diaphanes.com/titel/an-ecology-of-materials-3064 (accessed: 31 May 2019).

16 For more on this subject, see Karen Barad, 'Posthuman Performativity: Toward an Understanding of How Matter Comes to Matter', in *Journal of Women in Culture and Society* 28, no. 3 (2003): pp. 801–831; Karen Barad, *Meeting the Universe Halfway: Quantum Physics and the Entanglement of Matter and Meaning* (Durham and London: Duke University Press, 2007).

17 Alphonso Lingis, *The Imperative* (Bloomington and Indianapolis: Indiana University Press, 1998), pp. 76, 82, 121.

18 Michel Serres, *The Parasite* [1980], trans. Lawrence R. Schehr (Minnesota: University of Minnesota Press, 2007).

19 See, for example, Bruno Latour, *We Have Never Been Modern* [1991], trans. Catherine Porter (Cambridge and Massachusetts: Harvard University Press, 1993); Jane Bennett, *Vibrant Matter: A Political Ecology of Things* (Durham and London: Duke University Press, 2009).

20 Gertrude Stein, 'Poetry and Grammar', in *Lectures in America* (Boston: Beacon Press, 1985), pp. 209–246, here pp. 211–212.

21 *Doppelgänger (Walls With Flaws)*, 2013, Fig. pp. 14–16.

22 *Reassuring a Heater of Its Temperature*, 2014, Fig. pp. 52–54.

23 *Statiker*, 2013, Fig. p. 98.

24 *Soliloqui (yellow)*, 2016, Fig. p. 27.

25 *Frames*, 2018, Fig. pp. 22–26.

26 *Staircase*, 2011, Fig. p. 111.

27 *Sealed Vessels*, 2018, Fig. pp. 18–21, 91.

28 Rosalind E. Krauss, *Passages in Modern Sculpture* (New York: The Viking Press, 1977), p. 5.

29 Heidegger, 1950 (see note 1), p. 175.

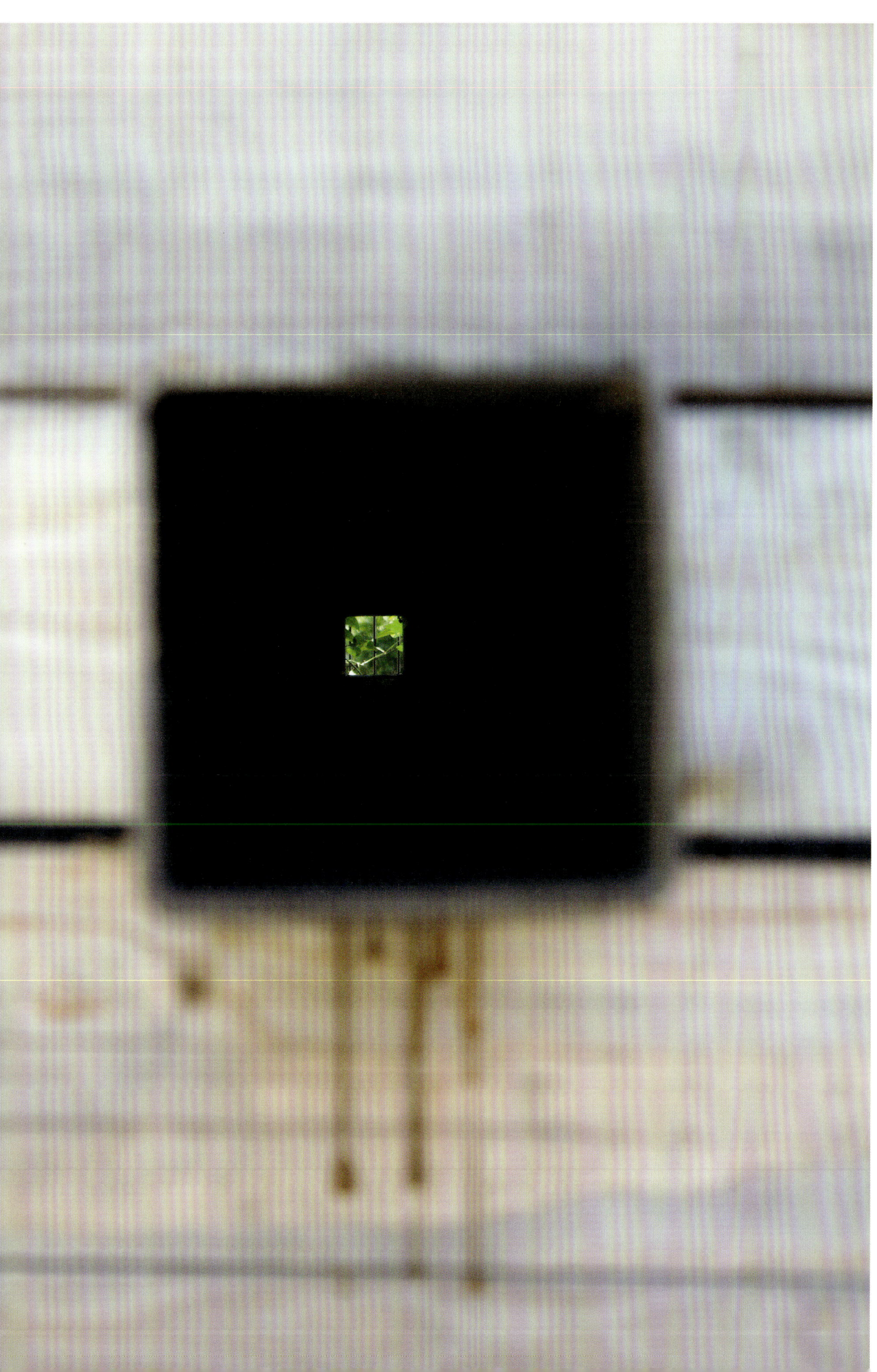

Blick durch Ozean (2013)
Vierkantrohr / square tube
12 × 12 × 600 cm

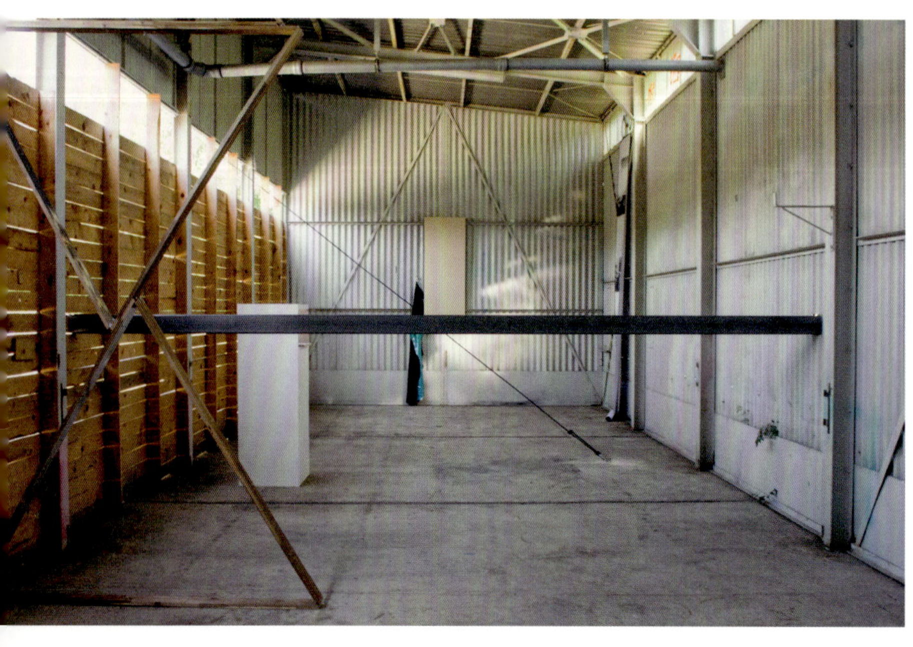

Ozean, Berlin 2013

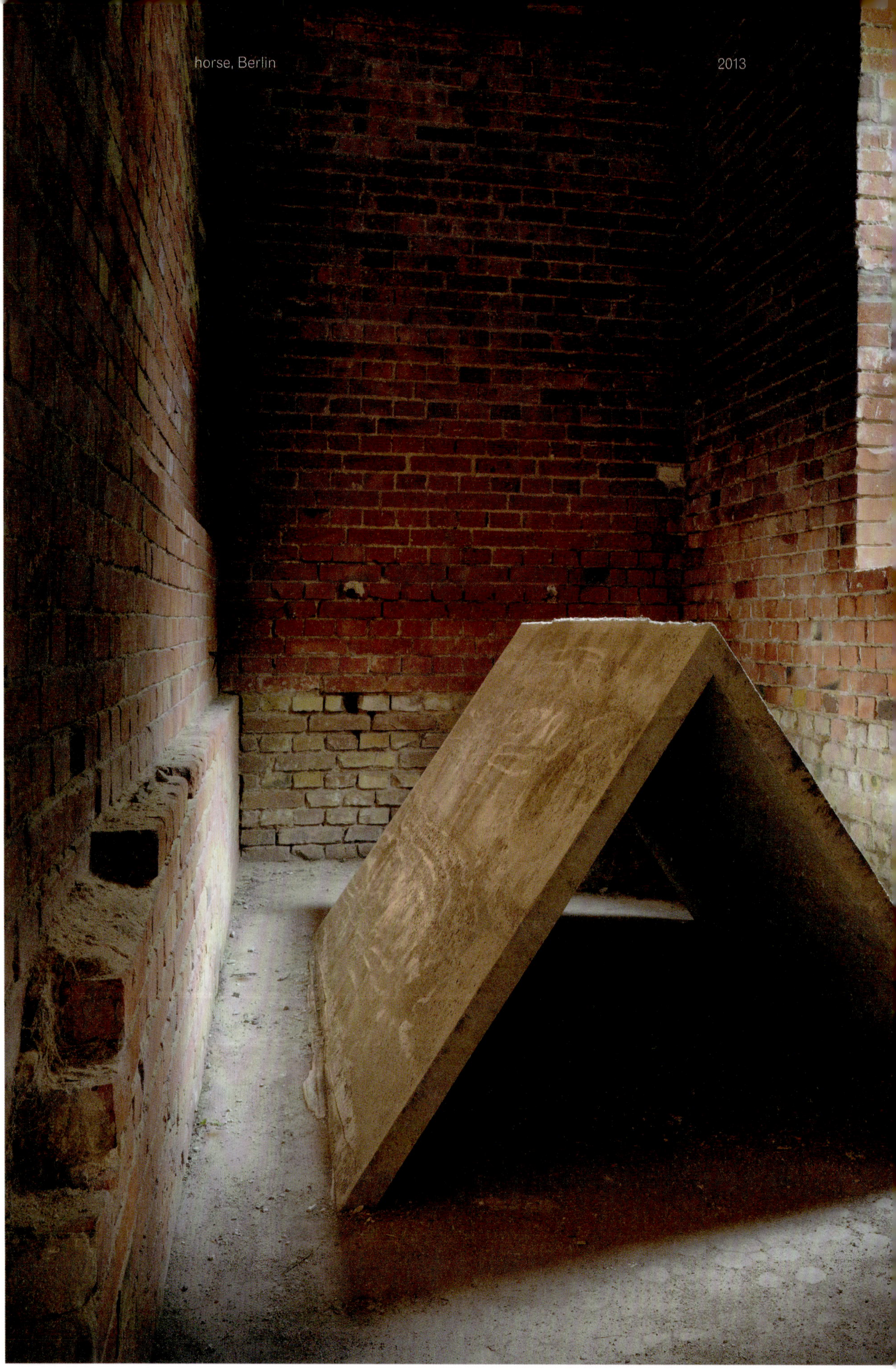

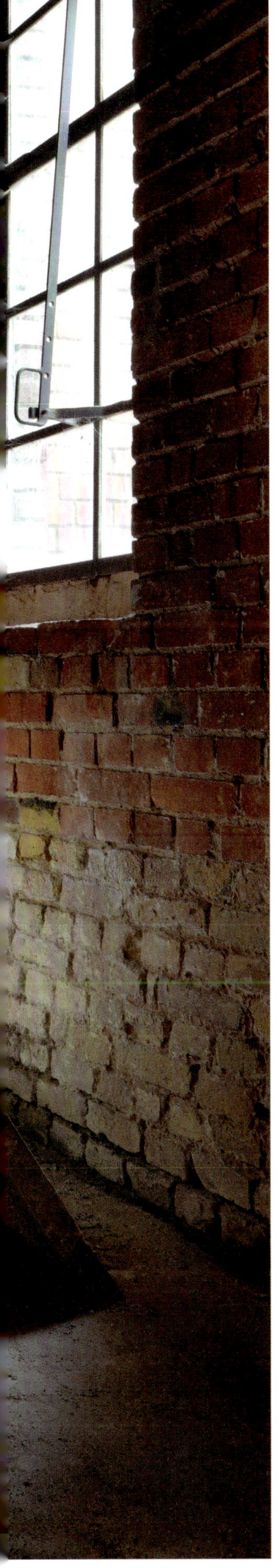

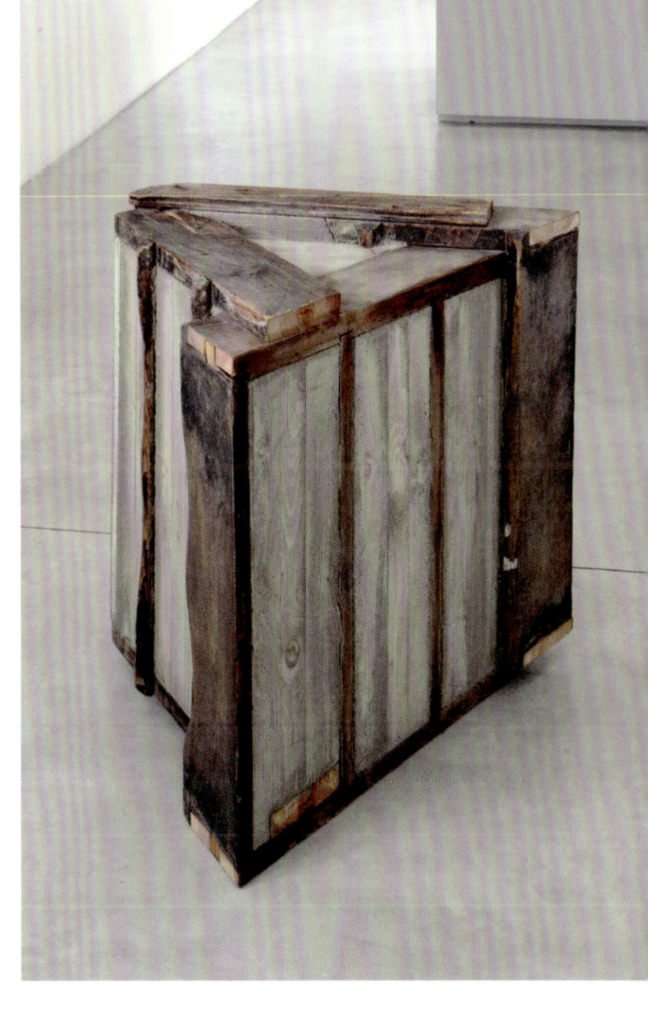

Treppe / Staircase (2011)
Holztreppe, Beton / wooden stairs, concrete
70 × 65 × 66 cm

Zelt / Tent (2013)
Stahlbeton / reinforced concrete
100 × 130 × 200 cm

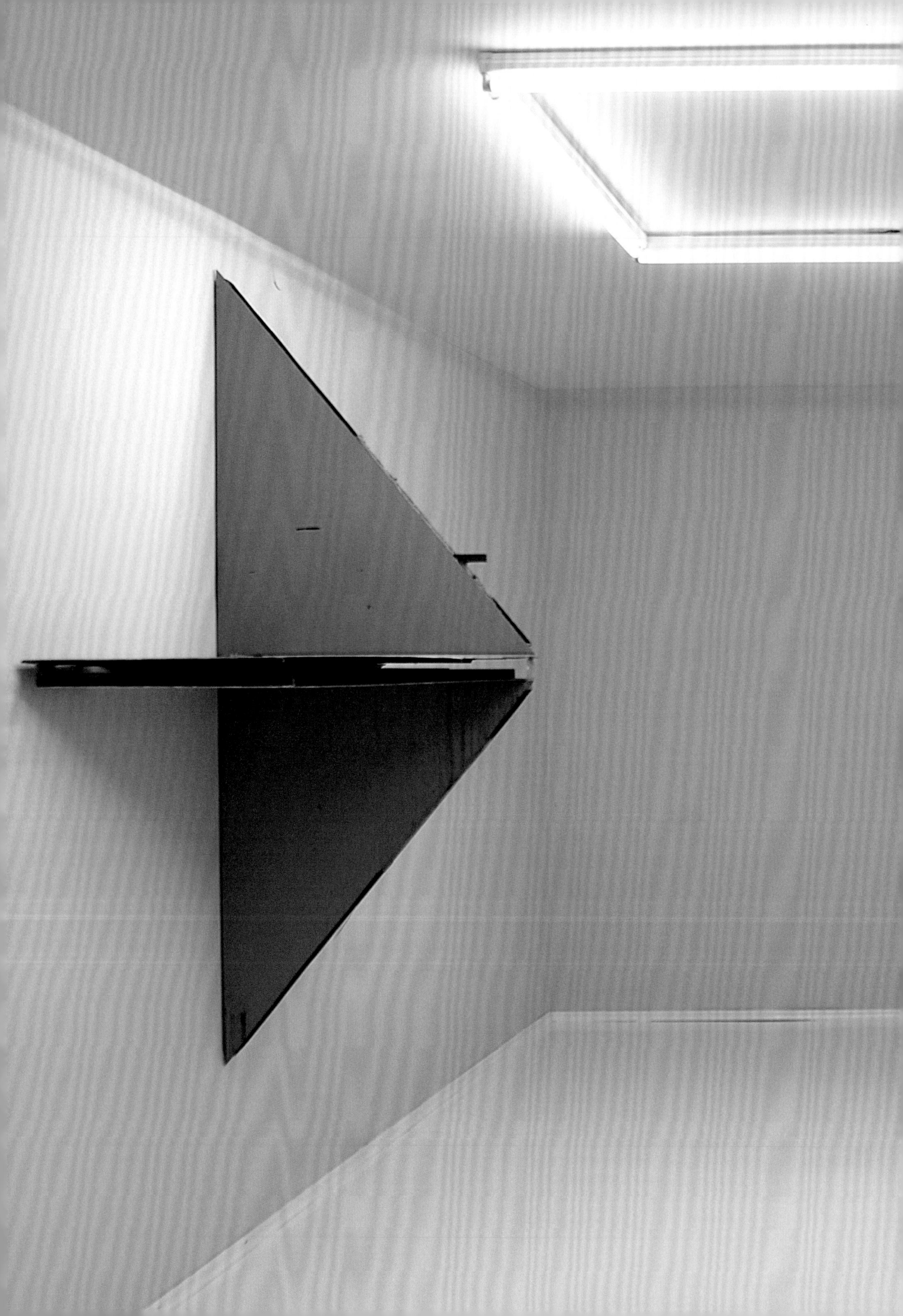

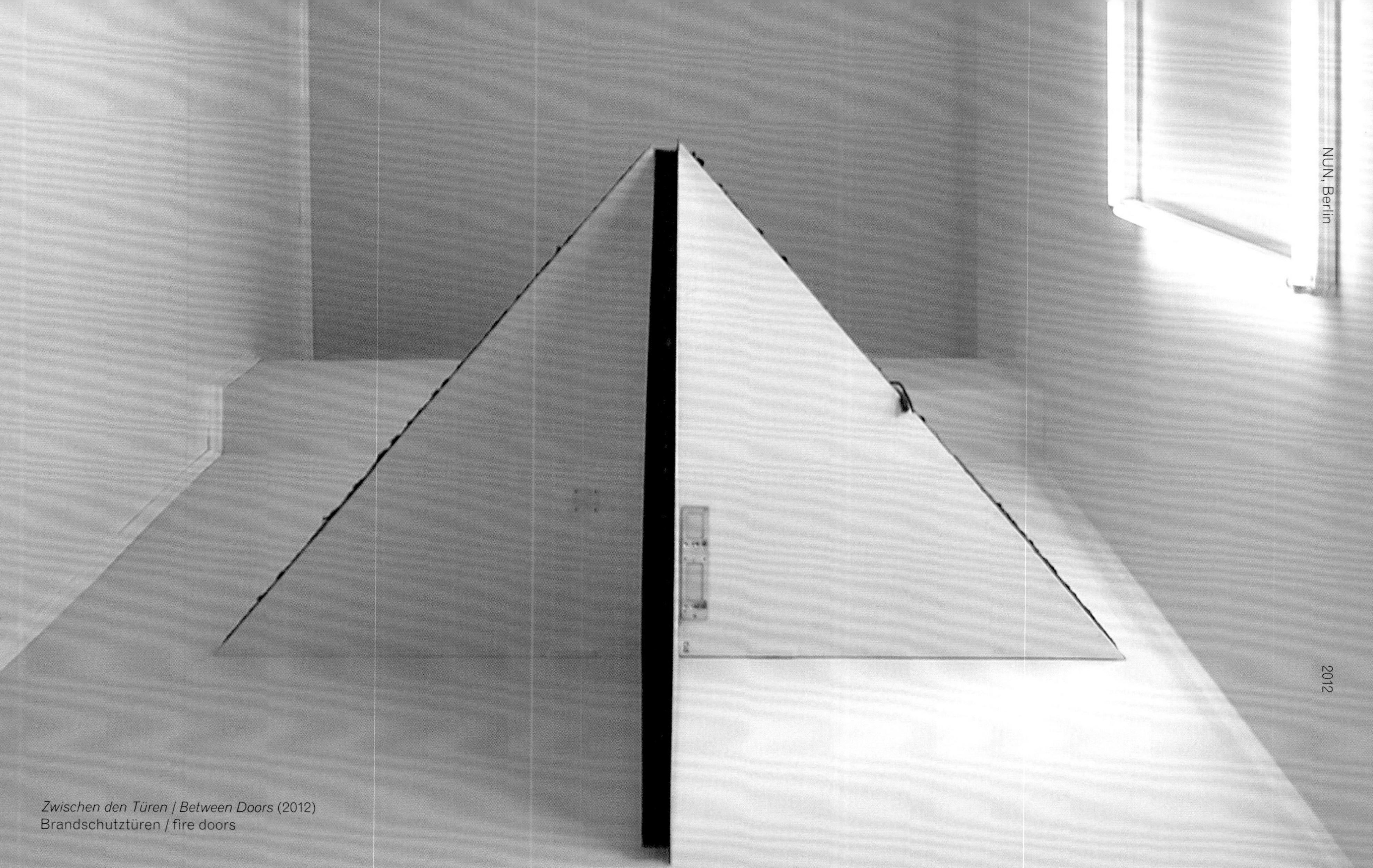

Zwischen den Türen / *Between Doors* (2012)
Brandschutztüren / fire doors

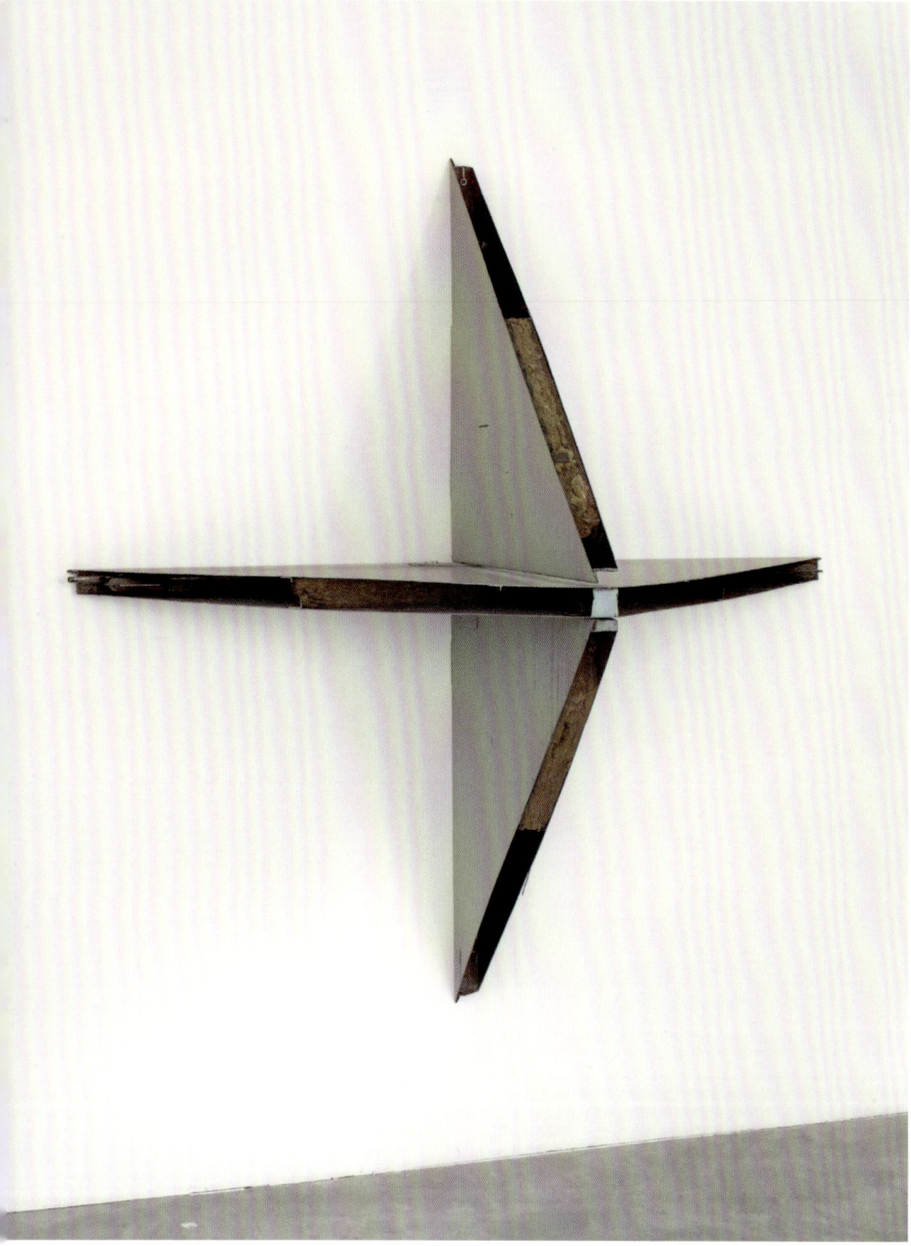

Im Nacken (2011)
Brandschutztür / fire door
210 × 217 × 92 cm

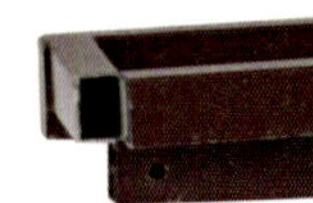

Cornered (2018)
Tischgestell / table frame
16 × 80 × 80 cm

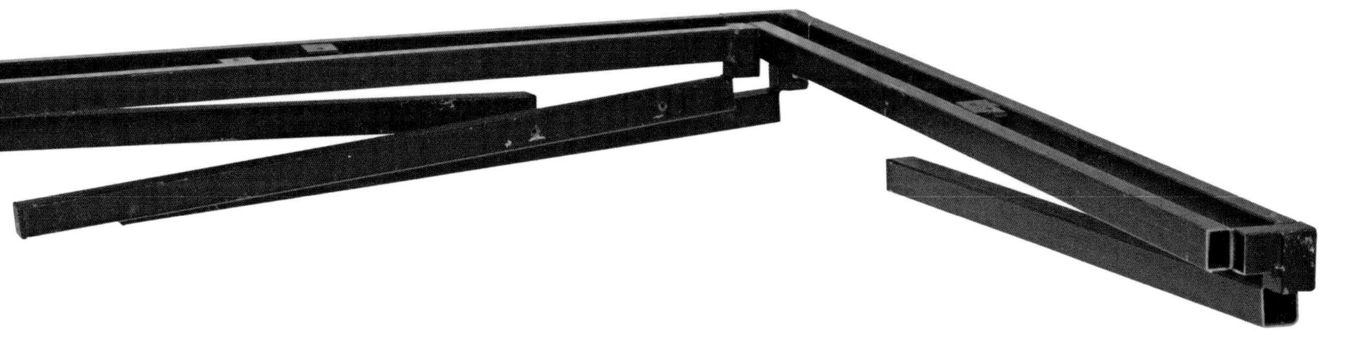

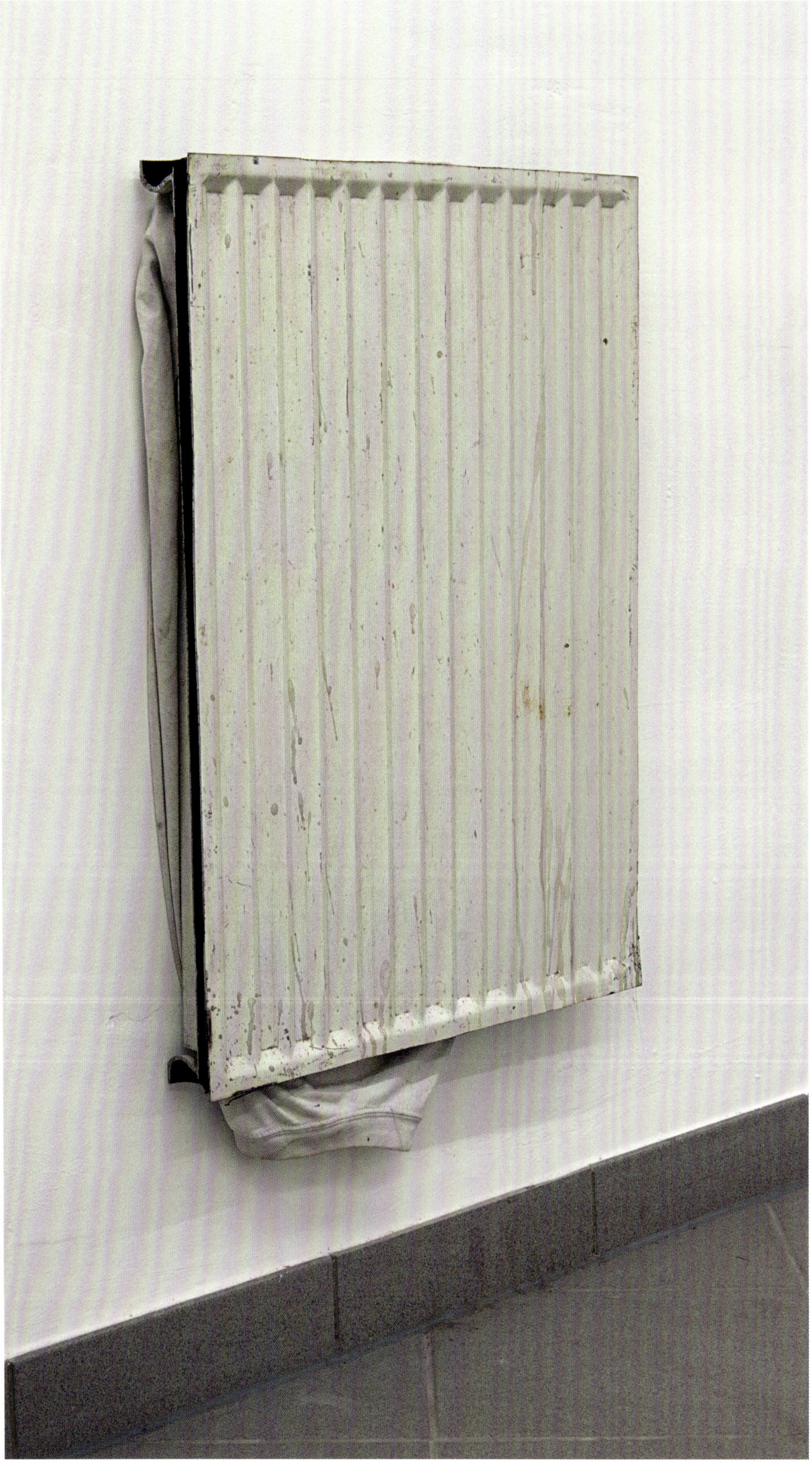

Heizkörper (2017)
Heizkörper, T-Shirt / heater, T-shirt
61 × 46 × 5 cm

Solo

2018 *Sealed Vessels*, The Gallery Apart, Rom / Rome, I **2017** *Closing Circuits*, Lichthaus Kunstverein Arnsberg, D • *Stray Currents*, The Gallery Apart, Rom / Rome, I • *Das Maß der Dinge*, mit / with Ingo Gerken, Galerie im Saalbau, Berlin, D **2015** *Vehikel*, Statsion, Berlin, D **2014** *The Gatekeeper (A Homeopathic Show)*, Another Space, Kopenhagen / Copenhagen, DK • *Soliloqui*, The Gallery Apart, Rom / Rome, I **2013** *Wechsel der Beleuchtung*, Espace Surplus Le Grand, Berlin, D • *Under the Weather*, mit / with Alona Rodeh, Hezi Cohen Gallery, Tel Aviv, IL • *Sich im Unendlichen kreuzende Parallelen*, mit / with Matthias Ströckel, seitenlichtsaal, Kunsthalle Düsseldorf, D **2012** *Zwischen den Türen*, NUN, Berlin, D • *Nothing succeeds like success, and nothing survives like survival*, Ozean, Berlin, D • *Florian Neufeldt*, ViennaFair, Wien / Vienna, A **2011** *Im Nacken*, Galerie Opdahl, Berlin, D • *Quelques coins et un cercle*, Rue de Tourtille, Paris, F **2010** *More Or The Same*, 26cc & The Gallery Apart, Rom / Rome, I • *Durchunddurch*, dreizehn / thirteen, Berlin, D • *Spot°light (SPTLT): FLORIAN NEUFELDT*, Galerie Nusser & Baumgart, München / Munich, D • *Cuts both Ways*, Galleri Opdahl, Stavanger, N **2009** *Planke*, Praterstraße 48, Wien / Vienna, A • *I and it, it and I*, Galerie Opdahl, Berlin, D **2008** *dix-huit*, mit / with Constantin Wallhäuser, Espace Surplus, Berlin, D • *Maschine*, Parrotta Project Space, Berlin, D **2007** *cinque*, mit / with Simon Menner, Espace Surplus, Berlin, D

Gruppe / Group

2018 *A Full Stomach in Zero Gravity*, Galleri Opdahl, Stavanger, N • *Delicious Disarray*, Berlin weekly, D **2017** *Herbstsalon*, Victor Hugo, Berlin, D • *Nischenhain*, Simultanhalle, Köln / Cologne, D **2016** *Regulars, Actually*, Galleri Opdahl, Stavanger, N • *Kunstpreis Haus am Kleistpark*, Berlin, D • *Geheimnis*, Kunstverein Kunsthaus Potsdam, D • *Höhenrausch*, Eigen & Art Lab, Berlin, D **2015** *Self-Storage, Another Space*, Kopenhagen / Copenhagen, DK • *Mappa dell'arte nuova, Imago Mundi – Luciano Benetton Collection*, Fondazione Cini di Venezia, Venedig / Venice, I • *Xerox*, Bar Babette, Berlin, D • *Blue Moon*, Kunsthalle Duderstadt, D • *Locker out of Order*, oqbo, Berlin, D **2014** *The Circular Ruins*, The Meet Factory, Prag / Prague, CZ **2013** *homecomings*, horse, Berlin, D • *Schweben?*, oqbo, Berlin, D • *parasite*, Ozean, Berlin, D **2012** *Florian Neufeldt, Philipp Leissing und Martin Roth*, Ve.sch, Wien / Vienna, A • *ILOVIT*, Copenhagen Art Festival, DK • *Kunstresidenz Bad Gastein*, A • *Mesmerized*, Galerie Opdahl, Berlin, D • *The dog days of entropy*, Nationalmuseum, Berlin, D • *Die Leidenschaften. Ein Drama in 5 Akten*, kuratiert von / curated by Catherine Nichols, Deutsches Hygiene-Museum, Dresden, D **2011** *Hear Me Out*, kuratiert von / curated by Cecilia Casorati, CIAC Museum, Genazzano, I • *Uncanny Valley / Unvertrautes Heim*, kuratiert von / curated by Marcel Schumacher und / and Britt Baumann, Architektursommer Rhein-Main 2011, Offenbach, D • *Gruppenausstellung. Praterstraße Berlin*, kuratiert von / curated by Leslie Weißgerber, Praterstraße Berlin, D • *Site*, kuratiert von / curated by Katja Dietrich-Kröck und / and Catherine Nichols, Kunstraum Potsdam, D • *KOH-I-NOOR*, Den Frie – Centre of Contemporary Art, Kopenhagen / Copenhagen, DK **2010** *On a Boat*, kuratiert von / curated by Sandra Teitge, Boot Helene, Berlin, D • *Curated Sculpture*, kuratiert von / curated by Pedro Wirz und / and Michael Birchall, Galerie Parrotta, Stuttgart, D • *Plus. Vorübergehender Überschuss*, kuratiert von / curated by Bettina Springer, Espace Surplus, Berlin, D • *Circus Hein*, Open Space, Art Cologne, Köln / Cologne, D • *Circle Work*, Parkhaus, Berlin, D • *dreizehn / thirteen. Praeludium. a group show*, dreizehn / thirteen, Berlin, D • *Fröhliche Gesellschaft. Editionen*, Centre d'Édition Contemporaine, Genf / Geneva, CH und / and Galerie Parrotta, Stuttgart, D **2009** *Circus Hein*, kuratiert von / curated by Jeppe Hein, Atelier Alexander Calder, Saché und / and FRAC, Orléans, F • *Site Specific! Zur Ortsspezifizität junger Positionen*, kuratiert von / curated by Bettina Springer, Kunstverein Kunsthaus Potsdam, D • *State of the Art*, Art Copenhagen, DK • *Continuous Perspectives #2*, Galerie Nusser & Baumgart, Leipzig, D • *Aus der Tiefe des Raumes*, Institut Rheinumschlag, Düsseldorf, D **2008** *11 Nullen*, Danziger Straße 146, Berlin, D • *Kunst und Babys*, Maxim, Köln / Cologne, D • *Mit Heissen Nadeln*, Geh8, Dresden, D **2007** *Maschine*, Parrotta Contemporary Art, Stuttgart, D • *Into the Woods Tonight*, Parrotta Project Space, Berlin, D • *Into the Woods Tonight*, Parrotta Contemporary Art, Stuttgart, D • *Jeppe empfiehlt: Vorschub*, kuratiert von / curated by Jeppe Hein, Schlosserei Vorschub, Berlin, D

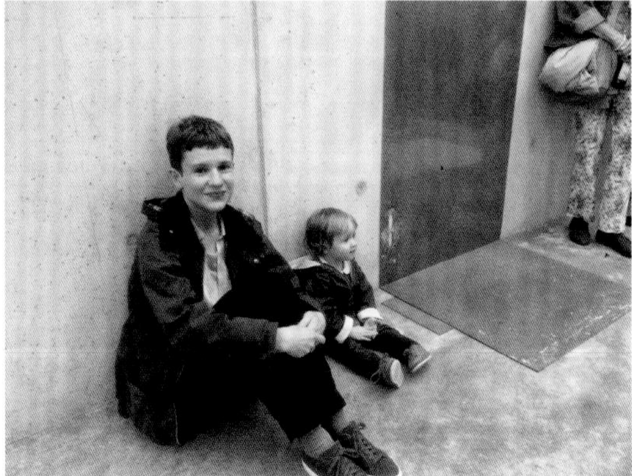

Stipendien / Scholarships

2019 TOKAS, Tokio / Tokyo, JP, Aufenthaltsstipendium des Berliner Senats / Residency Programme of the Berlin Senate **2017** Katalogförderung / Catalogue Funding, Stiftung Kunstfonds, Bonn **2014** SOArt Residency, Großegg, A **2012** Kunstresidenz / Art Residency, Bad Gastein, A **2011** Arbeitsstipendium / Work Scholarship, Stiftung Kunstfonds, Bonn **2010** Cité Internationale des Arts, Paris, F, Aufenthaltsstipendium des Berliner Senats / Residency Programme of the Berlin Senate

Florian Neufeldt

1976	in Bonn geboren, arbeitet und lebt in Berlin / born in Bonn, works and lives in Berlin
1997–1999	Kunstakademie Düsseldorf / Art Academy Düsseldorf
1999–2005	Studium der Soziologie in Köln und Berlin / studies of sociology in Cologne and Berlin

Impressum / Colophon

Konzeption / Concept
Christin Kaiser, Florian Neufeldt

Gestaltung / Design
Christin Kaiser

Texte / Texts
Gerrit Gohlke, Catherine Nichols

Übersetzung / Translation
Ann Marie Bohan

Lektorat / Copy Editing
Cassandra Edlefsen Lasch, Almut Otto

Fotonachweis / Photo Credits
Giorgio Benni (S. / pp. 22–23, 33, 52–54), Bitmap (S. / pp. 90–91), Katharina Gossow (S. / p. 74), Katja Illner (S. / p. 60), Christin Kaiser (S. / p. 116), Pierre-Etienne Morelle (S. / pp. 112–113), Tal Nisim (S. / pp. 14–16), Jessica Schäfer (S. / pp. 66–67), Eric Tschernow (S. / pp. 72–73, 92, 111, 114), Marc Volk (S. / pp. 62–65), Jens Ziehe (S. / pp. 56–59, 110–111), Christof Zwiener (S. / p. 51)
Alle anderen Abbildungen / All other photos © Florian Neufeldt

Lithografie / Image Editing
Johann Hausstätter

Produktion / Production Management
DISTANZ Verlag

Gesamtherstellung / Printing and Binding
optimal media GmbH, Röbel/Müritz

Vertrieb / Distribution
edel Germany GmbH
www.edel.com
international-books@edel.com

ISBN 978-3-95476-296-5
Printed in Germany

Erschienen im / Published by
DISTANZ Verlag
www.distanz.de

Dank / Acknowledgments
Manuela du Bois-Reymond, Cassandra Edlefsen Lasch, Gerrit Gohlke, Julia Hansen, Johann Hausstätter, Holger Hübsch, Ulrike Kirsten, Birgit Möckel, Wilhelm Neufeldt, Catherine Nichols, Annette und Jürgen Niepelt, Arve Opdahl, Armando Porcari, Nikolai von Rosen, Christian und Renate Schweitzer, Fabrizio del Signore, Burkhardt Söll, Tia Villalobos und insbesondere / and above all C. K.

Gefördert durch die Stiftung Kunstfonds, Bonn

STIFTUNG KUNSTFONDS

Coverbild / cover image
Selbstgespräch / Soliloquy (2012)
Tischgestell / table frame
38 × 26 × 26 cm